Folklore in New World Black Fiction

෨

Folklore in New World Black Fiction

Writing and the Oral Traditional Aesthetics

∿

Chiji Akọma

THE OHIO STATE UNIVERSITY PRESS • Columbus

Library of Congress Cataloging-in-Publication Data
Akọma, Chiji.
 Folklore in New World Black fiction : writing and the oral traditional aesthetics
/ Chiji Akọma.
     p. cm.
 Includes bibliographical references (p.   ) and index.
 ISBN-13: 978-0-8142-1071-0 (cloth : alk. paper)
 ISBN-10: 0-8142-1071-6 (cloth : alk. paper)
1. American fiction—African American authors—History and criticism.
2. Literature and folklore—United States—History—20th century. 3. African
American oral tradition. 4. African Americans—Intellectual life. 5. African
Americans in literature. 6. Folklore in literature. 7. Hermeneutics. I. Title.
 PS374.N4A36 2007
 810.9'896073—dc22
                                2007017452

This book is available in the following editions:
Cloth (ISBN: 978-0-8142-1071-0)
CD-ROM (ISBN: 978-0-8142-9148-1)
Paper (ISBN: 978-0-8142-5703-6)
Cover design by Jenny Poff
Type set in SIL Gentium
Text design and typesetting by Juliet Williams

For Mama
Mandah Nwaorienma
Whose Cradle Still Rocks Me
And in Memory of Papa
Israel Enyinna
Who Taught Me Books Hum

.

— CONTENTS —

— ACKNOWLEDGMENTS —

This book is the product of several years of love, encouragement, frank criticism, and support that I received from a number of colleagues, teachers, mentors, friends, and relatives. Therefore, I would like to publicly thank all those who in various ways helped bring this work to fruition. I cannot but begin with my wife and friend, Musoba, who has been there since the inception of this project, obliging my every excuse to be away from home to work on a seemingly never-ending manuscript; and to our three children—Ke, Atamini, and Moyo—an exuberant bunch, never stinting in their admiration and love, often shown by playing on Daddy's papers strewn across the floor or by insisting on my telling them a folktale at the dinner table.

My deep gratitude to Professor Isidore Okpewho, my mentor, who from the first day I stepped into his graduate seminar at the University of Ibadan, Nigeria, to my years at Binghamton University, New York, and beyond, has shown undiminished interest in my professional advancement, modeling to me the pleasures and dignity of an active intellectual life, and here, reading several drafts of this manuscript. Needless to say that in writing this book, I have immensely benefited from Okpewho's vast body of scholarship on African oral performance aesthetics. I also thank Professors Carole Boyce Davies, Sidonie Smith, Philip Rogers, and Femi Taiwo for their keen endorsement of this project and offering me helpful suggestions toward its completion. And to these wonderful friends and colleagues from our days at Binghamton whose ears and eyes I can still count on in moments when the walk gets so steep—T. J. Anderson III, Pauline Kaldas, Miriam Gyimah, and Marcia Douglas, and special thanks to Pauline for her careful review of the earliest drafts of several of my writings. Let me also thank my colleagues Paul Steege, for reading a draft of the introduction, and Seth Koven, for pushing me toward the goal line. My thanks to the office of the Villanova University Vice President for Academic Affairs, for granting me a semester sabbatical that was very helpful to me during the revision process.

Some portions of this book have appeared as articles in journals. My thanks to the editors of the following journals: *Oral Tradition* for publishing my essay on Toni Morrison's *Paradise; The Caribbean Writer* for printing the essay on *Jonestown* by Wilson Harris; and *Research in African Literatures* for publishing a shorter version of the chapter on Roy Heath. I also offer my gratitude to the four authors whose works form the focus of this study for giving me the opportunity to explore their highly imaginative creations and cite them extensively. And here I must thank the folks at The Ohio State University Press, especially my editor, Ms. Sandy Crooms, whose interest in the project made the difference in getting it published, after all.

I am highly indebted to these family members: my sister Enyinne, brothers Alalazu, Felix, and Osondu, Sandra Solomon and son Antonio; Uncle Geoffrey and Aunt Mary Mwaungulu; Donald, Linda, Atu, Neema, and dear friends Scott and Taryn Anson, for their unparalleled emotional and spiritual support. To these great friends made through the years, Stephanie Shonekan, Ogochukwu Onwudiwe, David Mayinja, Doug Young, Mark Asuzu, Richard Mammah, and my Community Group at Covenant Fellowship Church, Glenn Mills, Pennsylvania, thank you for lifting me up in prayer when deadlines crashed upon me and writing became daunting.

Clearly, it takes a village to support the man who writes the book! In acknowledging the contributions of these individuals to the completion of this work, I also absolve them of whatever faults there are. Those remain firmly my sole responsibility. *Mmammanu-o!*

– ONE –

Black Oral Performance and Writing Traditions in the New World

The complexity of the New World demands that any meaningful exploration of its cultural landscape, especially with reference to its literary production, take note of the region's multiple racial identities, the histories of slavery, military conquests, and various forms of migration to the area in different times and circumstances. For a study on folkloric forms in narratives by writers of African descent in the New World, it is certainly important to bear that complexity in mind. Although this study draws heavily from African oral performance aesthetics in the examination of works by the selected authors, I am fully aware of the intersections between African folkloric practices and other cultural traditions that are present in these texts. Yet it is fair to claim a black bias based on the preponderance of signals indicative of that heritage and on the strength of the claims made by the authors. This point is worth emphasizing, for in a region composed of indigenous peoples and descendants of peoples from Africa, Asia, and Europe, it is tempting to view literary production through the prism of its most dominant member, the United States, which, despite the growing visibility of its minority writers, shares greater literary affinity with the West than with the rest of the Americas. Moreover, for much of the Southern Hemisphere that has long come under the political and economic dominance of the North and Europe, the ramifications of this dominance might be felt through the marginalization that occurs due to limited access to the world stage.

In the context of such dominance, many diasporic black writers have sought to assert their place in the New World's cultural production through conscious engagement with and tribute to their continental African heritage, a heritage largely defined by oral verbal arts and folklore. It is not difficult to assess the reason behind the close association between folklore and New World written narrative tradition. Africans brought in as slaves to work the plantations in the New World strove to maintain their religious and cultural bearing by relying on their memories of folk traditions in their various homelands and transforming them to usable and passable forms in the hostile Europeanized environment of the New World.

While the presence of folklore in contemporary black written narratives is not in doubt, what has not received adequate attention is the extent to which the folkloric tradition serves as the medium for engaging the works at a hermeneutic level. This book attempts to address this problem by adopting oral performance aesthetic values as its principal analytic tool for understanding select works by four prominent African New World novelists. In the New World literary tradition, folklore is not just a major aspect of the tradition, but for the works examined here, meaning is intrinsically connected with the oral strategies they embody.

Folk, Folklore, and the Folkloric Text

In conceptualizing folklore and the manner in which it is studied, it is important to see folklore as dynamic, adapting to the trends and sensibilities of a given group. This goes contrary to Paulo de Carvalho-Neto's argument in *The Concept of Folklore,* for example, where he tries to make a distinction between folklore and what he refers to as "aesthetic projection," which he defines as a "simulation of folklore . . . characterized by a change of transmitters, a change of motivation, a change of function, a change of forms, and a change of learning" (101). Put differently, he draws a distinction between "folklore" and "folklore lite." The idea that different degrees of "folklore" exist stems from his conceptualization of folklore as phenomenon "typified by being anonymous, non-institutionalized, and eventually by being ancient, functional, and prelogical" (82). One senses that Carvalho-Neto locates folklore among groups untouched by "civilization," while the rest of the world can only produce "simulated" folklore. The idea of "simulation" implicated in his "aesthetic projection" is a misunderstanding of the artistic imagination that inspires a performer and community in producing what is then received as folkloric. And what preserves a tradition if not the continuous imitation and re-presentation of that tradition by members of the community?

The essentialist bent of Carvalho-Neto is also evident in his argument about authorship and transmission. The folkloric act, he states, is such insofar as the originator is unknown. This position overstates the notion of communal/anonymous authorship related to oral traditions, as well as the connection between orality and antiquity. A pragmatic conceptualization of folklore would suggest that the social and cultural transformations that occur in human societies invariably bring about new and "original" compositions; such compositions are capable of bearing the stamp of individual ingenuity that does not undermine their status as communal artifacts. Besides, the prevalence of oral practices in antiquity does not and should not mean that folklore does not exist in contemporary societies.

On the other hand, Dan Ben-Amos rescues folklore from what seems like an atavistic view by defining it as performance. According to him, folklore is not merely an itemization of acts and thoughts but "a communicative process" (9). A folkloric act occurs when "both the performers and the audience have to be in the same situation and be part of the same reference group." He also notes that there has to be a "face to face" communication to make the act possible (12–13). The benefit of Ben-Amos's view is that it places the folkloric act in the field of cultural exchange between performer and audience. Both entities share a common cultural experience and the cultural transaction between them is mutually generated.

Nevertheless, Ben-Amos seems to lean too heavily on the communicative context of the folkloric act. To circumscribe the folkloric act within "face to face" exchange would be to ignore the other levels of orality that are possible. The performance of folklore in print, television, and other such mass media cannot be a basis for not recognizing an act as folklore. If Roger D. Abrahams's assertion that folklore "gives form to energies set in motion by some shared or social anxiety" ("Personal Power" 19) is valid, then the context of expressing "anxiety" cannot supersede the performance itself insofar as the folkloric transaction, in whatever medium, remains mutual between the participants. This view is made more cogent by the imperatives of social change; folklore resists "tradition" as it is constantly reflecting and refashioning the experience of the community, whether in antiquity or in posterity.

The artistry of folklore (i.e., its capacity to represent group consciousness through artistic expression) further suggests that the primary concern of the performers, and the assumption that informs the group's reception of the act, is the *quality* of the experience being evoked. To emphasize the point in relation to the present discussion, once folklore is separated from the narrow notion of being produced by "simple folk," a more fruitful discussion of its presence in contemporary New World black literature ensues. To open up possibilities for exploring the kinds of literatures produced in the New World, especially among writers of African descent, this work defines folklore as the gamut of cultural and literary production disseminated over oral, written, and electronic media that is inspired by a high degree of communal philosophy, ethos, or beliefs.

There are reasons for approaching the concept of folklore from a contemporaneous standpoint. First, it creates wider avenues for examining the subject. The term "folk" can no longer be restricted to the context of locality or social and economic class. As Alan Dundes posits, "'folk' can refer to *any group of people whatsoever* who share at least one common factor. It does not matter what the linking factor is—it could be a common occupation, language . . . but what is important is that a group formed for whatever reason will have some traditions which it calls its own" (2). Thus a reading, viewing, or listening audience spatially removed from the performer can constitute a group involved in a cultural transaction that has been transformed into an available contemporary medium. This book identifies the New World black narrative as a transmitter of the folkloric act. The configuration of this act through the interplay of oral and written signs forms the central concern of my study. In narrative, there still exists an identifiable cultural space where the novelists and their audience in the Americas engage in a folkloric transaction with an empathy not unlike that of face-to-face interchange in oral groups. As I shall try to demonstrate, the Afro-diasporic novelist engages in the folkloric act with an awareness of the community's traditions similar to that of an oral performer. The difference is that the written context of transmission inevitably requires different parameters for the signification of the folkloric act. This difference is not a devaluation of the act. The challenge facing the scholar is to evaluate the folkloric act in its transformed identity, as artists and community respond to a rapidly technologizing world.

Africa and New World Consciousness

Earlier, I referred to the African diaspora as a single cultural space. This is arguably misleading, for while diaspora black culture may be said to originate from a common African ancestry, the social, political, and economic peculiarities discernible in the various geographical spaces occupied by the diaspora demand an appropriate sensitivity to differences.[1] Thus, in the matter of the folkloric act and the New World black narrative, it is necessary to pay attention to the different views on aesthetics of blacks on both sides of the Atlantic. Bearing this in mind, David Dorsey's definition of black aesthetics as "the syndrome of internal factors governing a black audience's perception and appreciation of art" (7) may be useful in distinguishing aesthetics in racial terms, but not adequate in analyzing the specificities of regional identities that make up what we refer to as the African diaspora. Certainly, black aesthetics may be assumed to exclude nonblack communities. However, considering the historical circumstances that have transformed black peoples in global contexts, it is doubtful that a serious discussion on Afro-diasporic aesthetics can be sustained where the category "black" is pressed to the disregard of difference. Surely, there exists some difference between, say, Chinua Achebe's and Wole Soyinka's conceptualizations of the black aesthetic on the one hand, and James Baldwin's and Richard Wright's on the other.[2] An awareness of such differences will guide the emphasis I intend to place on African New World experiences and discourses, rather than the more tempting option of pursuing the folkloric act in the New World from an entirely African viewpoint.[3] And by African, I refer principally to the Atlantic West Coast, where the majority of blacks in the New World trace their lineage and cultural heritage.[4]

In his essay "The African Imagination," Abiola Irele identifies the spoken word as the informing sensibility of literary expression in Africa. Not only is oral literature a medium but, indeed, the corpus of artistic expressions in the continent derives its durability from, and is sustained by, the nature of oral discourse. Hence, Irele concludes that orality is the "basic intertext of the African imagination" (56). Whatever we identify as African literature is derived mainly from the creative dynamics generated by the oral form. The "aesthetic transaction" to which Ropo Sekoni refers in his *Folk Poetics* is based on an interaction between an audience and a performer operating in an oral context (10). The audience and the performer know each other, and both recognize that the artist is working with materials generated through communal cultural consciousness. Even where the performer is transformed into a writer, with the attendant solitariness and individuality that go with the writing process, one finds that in many instances the writer still lays claim to a communal ethos shared with the readership.[5] I cannot emphasize enough this necessity for affinity between performer and audience because that relationship is connected to the spoken word, a phenomenon that deserves further explanation.

The spoken word does not derive its primacy merely because of the prevalence of primary orality in parts of the continent. Among the Dogon of Mali, for example, the creative principle in Amma, the godhead, is embodied in Nommo, the power of speech. Achebe's often-cited authorial comment in *Things Fall Apart* that the art of conversation is highly regarded among the Igbo of Nigeria (7) could also be said about other African ethnic groups. In many African societies, the speech act is a ceremony, an occasion for the display of several levels of artistic showmanship that is an important element in the aesthetics of the group. The ample investment in the spoken word, especially at the literary level, is due to the immense performative force of the speech act. In performance, the artist undertakes complementary kinesic acts that distinguish his or her competence from that of others. These kinesic acts include modulation of voice, dance steps that accompany singing, the interactive gestures the artist makes with the audience, and the facial expressions (including eye movements) that accompany each spoken word. The performance of the spoken word is an occasion for a theatrical assemblage that tasks the creative talent of the performer while satisfying the audience's demand for a visually and aurally pleasing reinforcement of their artistic heritage.

Furthermore, the eminence given to the spoken word is not only in the opportunity it provides for a sense of theater in performance. Speech is also the agency through which the literary "canons" of the society are reinforced, extended, recreated, and even, logically, created. Built into the aesthetic of the African oral performance is the expectation that the performance would generate a new "tome" to be added to the larger repertoire. The community does not gather to hear and watch what they have heard and seen before; the artistic appreciation of each performance involves the observance of the degree to which the performer has made a peculiar imprint on the material drawn from the common repertoire. What constitutes the repertoire of the community and, by extension, what defines the community's artistic values is constantly negotiated between the audience and the artist. Such a continual mediation traditionally takes place in the context of the oral performance where the spoken word holds sway, and where each constituted audience is the guardian of the tradition. The significance of the negotiation is what Isidore Okpewho suggests when he says of the nature of oral composition, "it always involves some amount of compromise between tried and tested techniques and new elements invented or substituted for a specific occasion or purpose. . . . The ready-made phrase or pattern of procedure . . . is now combined with new elements . . . and a new song or tale is born" (*African Oral Literature* 33).

These fundamental principles of the African oral performance also apply to written literature. True, the interactive moments of oral performance are not realizable in print; however, African writers pursue the same aesthetic goals through representing the essence of such values. A performance-driven aesthetic mediates the oral tradition and the relatively younger written tradition. A reading of Yambo Ouologuem's *Bound to Violence* or Ngugi's *Petals of Blood,* along with more recent works, reveals how some African writers manipulate language and cultural context in order to satisfy the oral performance demand to show competence through verbal dexterity.[6]

In addition to the performative aspect of the oral art, the African aesthetic principle also derives from a connection of art with the physical environment. Okpewho has referred to this situation as the "ecology of art" (*Epic* 19). One of the examples he uses to buttress his point is a reference to D. T. Niane's *Sundiata: An Epic of Old Mali.* There, the griot of Sundiata's father chides the hunter-seer for the obscurity of his prophesy, charging him to "speak in the language of your Savanna" (ibid.). The royal griot seems to be pointing to the unacceptability of art that does not reflect the environment of its community. In the same book, Okpewho demonstrates how difference in the physical landscapes of various African regions is responsible for the prominence or absence of certain narrative tropes across the continent (19–21). Thus, the content of the speech form is reflective of the texture of the environment. Similarly, in the New World black writing experience, one observes the effort of artists or critics to represent their condition through metaphors drawn from their environment. For example, some African Caribbean writers have attempted to articulate their community's reality through the metaphor of maroonage, a metaphor that interlocks with the landscape of a strange island and a threatening sea.

In the Americas, the articulation of the black aesthetic has been both simple and complicated: simple in that blacks in the Americas are historically known to be descendants of Africans captured as slaves and forcefully brought to the New World. At this level, discussion of the black aesthetic has understandably prioritized its African roots and has sometimes even dismissed the possibility of articulating it along other lines. For example, John O'Neal, one of the critics of the 1960s Black Arts movement, argued that African Americans must see themselves as Africans and not as Americans (47–48). In that vein, the aesthetic philosophy expounded takes its bearing, or tries to do so, from an African model. In his work dealing with the corn-shucking activity in slave plantations, *Singing the Master*, Roger D. Abrahams has argued that though the slaves "developed uniquely American traditions of interacting, celebrating and worshipping," such traditions were mainly "organized around the moral and aesthetic principles found throughout much of the sub-Saharan world from which they came" (xviii). Using the corn-shucking event as a paradigm, Abrahams reveals how the performance aspects of the ceremony indicate their African origins and how these aspects have been critical to the formulation of black aesthetics in the Americas, especially in the United States. One of the characteristics is the antiphonality involved in the call and response and its effectiveness in guaranteeing universal participation.

There is also the dance element Abrahams identifies as "cutting," a competitive process involving "a cutting up, a breaking away from the group, with the dancer making a bid for attention as he 'shows his stuff' or as she 'makes her motion' to the others" (101). Closely related to "cutting" is "breaking"; but here the emphasis is not so much on establishing difference from the "norm" as on accentuating the "strangeness of the alteration" (102).[7]

Other artistic aspects of the corn-shucking activity are the audience that forms a ring around the dancer, the group leader elected because of his eloquence and ability to improvise, and the songs intricately deployed as vocal accompaniment to manual work. These close affinities to African oral performance lead Abrahams to make an important statement: "traditional features of African eloquence and improvisation in speech, song, and dance provided the basis for the development of an Afro-American aesthetic system which has been maintained to this day" (130). Although he does not underrate the considerable influence of European culture on blacks, Abrahams's study clearly situates the core of the African American aesthetic in an African paradigm.

On the other hand, writers and critics such as James Baldwin, Carole Boyce Davies, and Paul Gilroy at different times have interrogated the validity of overemphasizing the African antecedent of the aesthetics of blacks in the diaspora. The problem begins with the concept of the "African Diaspora." How African can the later generations of former African slaves in the New World claim to be after such an extensive association with the whites and Indians of the Americas? With the shifting migration patterns among blacks in the New World and Europe, to what extent can the notion of essential "blackness" be pursued in these multicultural sites?

These questions become more cogent by the ascendancy of Afrocentric discourse in many U.S. colleges, whereby Africans and blacks in the diaspora are viewed as operating within a homogeneous ontological space. But as Carole Boyce Davies has argued, albeit from a black feminist perspective, any totalizing view of the black experience (or "African-diaspora") direly needs to be interrogated, especially when linked with a masculinist notion of nationalism. In her words,

> Any articulation of a critique of home for Black women has to begin with an examination of the totalizing nature of nationalist (Africa-diaspora) discourse. Pan-Africanism, Black/African nationalism and Afrocentricity are "totalizing discourses" which can tolerate no different articulation and operate from a singularly monolithic construction of an African theoretical homeland which asks for the submergence or silencing of gender, sexuality or any other ideological stance or identity position which is not subsumed under Black/African nationalism. (49–50)

Central to Davies's position is the conceptualization of "home." A broader notion of "home," she suggests, would include recognition of the diverse sociocultural and political experiences that have characterized peoples of African descent around the world. Africa and its aesthetic become an "imaginary/historical basis of identity or self-assertion" that shares equal significance with other ideas of "home" constructed along lines of gender, sexuality, or national territory (51).

Davies at least acknowledges the relevance of an African foundation (even if it is an imaginary one) while constructing other "homes." The British culture theorist Paul Gilroy dismisses even this minimal connection, claiming that "the term 'diaspora' . . . points emphatically to the fact that there can be no pure, uncontaminated, or essential blackness anchored in an unsullied originary moment" (*Small Acts* 99). Forceful as this assertion is, its usefulness is diminished in the extremity of that stance, for the presence of blacks in the Americas and Europe can be historically accounted for. I have already cited one concrete example in Hall's work where the ethnic identities of many of the Africans shipped to the Americas were documented in detail. Nor is it possible to dismiss as entirely unfounded an aesthetic that in broad terms explains some of the shared cultural categories existing both in Africa and in Afro-diasporic communities.

In *The Black Atlantic*, Gilroy attempts to articulate his notion of the African diaspora in what he terms the "Black Atlantic" with "The Ship" as its metaphor. The Black Atlantic, Gilroy argues, is "the rhizomorphic, fractal structure of the transcultural, international formulation," different from what he considers the "nationalistic focus" of cultural studies among the English and African Americans (4). Gilroy posits, "The image of the ship—a living, micro-cultural, micro-political system in motion—is especially important for historical and theoretical reasons [as] ships immediately focus attention on the middle passage, on the various projects for redemptive return to an African homeland" (4). Later in the work Gilroy specifies that the Black Atlantic construct is aimed at transcending "both the structures of the nation state and the constraints of ethnicity, and national particularity" (19).

The postmodernist fervor of Gilroy's argument is obvious. The idea of a ship floating in an ever-unfolding centerless ("rhizomorphic") space, and lacking a concrete structure, or rather, possessing a "fractal" one, makes for a fine theoretical expedition. Besides, it demands a discarding of presumptions about how cultural or political spaces operate in the predeconstructionist ideologies. We are called to recognize that indeed a space exists in which the historical, cultural, and political experience of blacks in the diaspora could be interrogated outside an African "fore-figure." But who gains from this proposition, and does the problem it seeks to solve really exist? Gilroy's premise for this fractal image of the diasporic African centers on the notion that Africans' cultural encounters, in their forced or voluntary sojourns in Europe and the Americas, have bequeathed on them "two great cultural assemblages" that are "locked symbiotically in an antagonistic relationship marked out by the symbolism of colors which adds to the conspicuous cultural power of their central Manichean dynamic—black and white" (*Black Atlantic* 1–2). Thus, diaspora consciousness is marked by angst, an eternal struggle of two traditions without resolution. But as Michael J. C. Echeruo ponders, while addressing this particular claim by Gilroy, "why should this particular plague be visited on black people? Why is it that creolisation is always an event attachable only to one of the two sources of hybridity? . . . Why is it that Europe, for all the changes and transformations it has undergone over the centuries, has remained a recognizable entity, whereas Africa . . . is always the sufferer, and its children the natural victims of this unique mental disorder of double consciousness?" (6). Echeruo raises poignant questions regarding the rush to neutralize the ontological and historical connection between Africa and Africans in the diaspora. Other groups that have experienced dispersion, notably, the Jewish people, never question their core Jewish identity no matter the cultural, linguistic, or political tensions that confront them where they sojourn. Thus, Gilroy's fractal construct proceeds from a faulty notion of diaspora identity.

To take the subject further, if such a rhizomorphic space exists, what do we make of a Black Atlantic that ignores ethnic particularities? The New World and Europe remain racialized and ethnically stratified territories. Race and ethnicity remain at the heart of many of the world's intractable conflicts, indicating how profound in people's lives they are. So, is it viable to efface ethnic differences and latch onto a floating ship with no clear idea of its ports of departure and arrival? Gilroy's Black Atlantic seems to gloss over the particularities of the experiences of blacks in the diaspora. Despite the shared experience of slavery between African Americans, from, say, Guyana and the United States, there are marked cultural and political differences.[8] Nation/state/nationality may be regarded as modern Western constructs by which blacks by virtue of the circumstances of their journey out of their homeland need not be constrained. Yet they are the emblems that distinguish the political expression of the American black from, say, the British black.

The notion of the Black Atlantic turns suspicious when an undercurrent of white supremacist thinking seems to be running through its rhetoric. In *Small Acts,* Gilroy proposes an aesthetic he calls "populist modernism," a term that, by his definition, shows the subordination of black art and politics under Western modernist thought and practice. According to him, populist modernism is a "distinctive aesthetic and ethico-political approach [that] requires a special gloss on terms like reason, justice, freedom and 'communicative ethics.'" He continues, "It starts from recognition of the African diaspora's peculiar position as 'step-children' of the West and of the extent to which our imaginations are conditioned by an enduring proximity to regimes of racial terror" (103). Though he refers to W. E. B. DuBois's famous notion of double-consciousness (8), what he fails to recognize, or perhaps chooses to ignore, is that DuBois's concept does not hierarchize the two shades of cultural consciousness the African in the New World embodies, as he (Gilroy) does by referring to diasporic blacks as stepchildren of the West—the quotation marks notwithstanding.[9] The inferiorization of an African consciousness, whether imaginary, as precondition for articulating a so-called liberatory African diasporic discourse, raises questions on the sincerity of such a project and equally calls for a scrutiny of whose interest is served in the process.[10]

Orality and Literacy

Considerable scholarship has been produced in the field of orality and its relationship to literacy. In the past fifty years or so, oral literary specialists have been engaged in exploring the connection between the oral performance of literature and the production of its written counterpart. Scholars such as Albert Lord, Walter Ong, Dell Hymes, Dennis Tedlock, Isidore Okpewho, Deborah Tannen, John Foley, Ruth Finnegan, and Elizabeth Fine have raised questions or attempted to answer questions, related to these interconnections. Their research has considered some of the following issues: To what extent is the epic genre a function of orality? What constitutes the oral imagination? What is the nature of the association between the oral performance as a text and the written representation of this text? How far can we attempt to establish a relationship between the dynamic nature of the oral performance and the fixed space wherein the written narrative is composed? Certainly, there are no clear-cut answers. Rather, what scholars have done is to discuss the issues with specific applications.

For anthropologists, folklorists, literary critics, and creative writers, these issues are pertinent in analyzing and (re)defining the process of literary production and transmission. In the African literary experience, the distinctions between literacy and orality also have a political dimension because of slavery and colonialism. The European colonizer, armed with a notion of cultural superiority (and a gun to enforce that belief on the colonized, to boot), promoted a new set of social and economic values based on literacy. In the process, the prevalent traditional oral arts were suppressed as products of a bygone, barbaric age, while the new class of Africans literate in the colonizer's language was taught with novels, poems, and, in some places, the Bible as models of "literature." The enthronement of Western literacy in the African colonies created a mistaken impression that literacy was synonymous with civilization, even though as early as 3000 BCE, ancient Egypt had developed a pictographic form of writing (hieroglyphics) that was to hold sway for the next two thousand years.[11] By being attached to the idea of civilization, literacy became an index of cultural and intellectual refinement.[12]

In *Interfaces of the Word*, Walter Ong argues that the rise of empiricist-scientific consciousness is traceable to the alienation of verbal performance from the speaker. Ong roots the consciousness (especially as it relates to the West) in the way certain languages, Latin, for example, originally a natural human oral verbalization acquired through nurture ("mother-tongue"), gradually became an exclusive and gender-discriminatory language, what he calls "Learned Latin" (25). The shift of medium of acquisition from mother to child through the spoken word to its appropriation in the formal all-male classroom through rules of writing effectively weakened the oral attribute. The development of the language no longer depended on the way it was spoken but on the way it was written. "This is a strange situation for a language," Ong remarks. "Latin was distanced—alienated—not from day-to-day life, for it was of the substance of daily life for lawyers, physicians, academic educators, and clergymen, but from the psychological roots of consciousness. It no longer in any sense belonged to mother. It did not come from where you came from" (28).

It is important to stress Ong's idea of alienation, for through it he pursues the connection of the written word with science—at least early modern science. With individuation, it was logical that the needs of science—the "need to hold at arm's length the human lifeworld with its passionate, rhetorical, practical concerns"—were readily met by written learned Latin (35). From being an ordinary chirographic signifier for the spoken language, writing became linked with cognitive capability. A similar thread of discussion runs in Eric Havelock's *Preface to Plato*. Havelock provides valuable insight through his reading of Plato's *Republic* in charting the course of the ancient Greeks' departure from the dialogic world of the spoken word to the monologic and "silent" discourse of writing. Education received during Homer's time and after relied on the ability to memorize (itself monologic) and perform the rhythmic epic narratives considered as a *paideia*, embodying the totality of Greek life and culture. Commenting on the significance of this form of education, Havelock writes: "Its [rhythmic narrative—epic] acceptance and retention are made psychologically possible by a mechanism of self-surrender to the poetic performance, and self-identification with the situations and the stories related in the performance. Only when the spell is fully effective can its mnemonic powers be fully mobilized" (198–99). It was an oral-aural pedagogical technique in which knowledge, or the ability to know, could not be separated from the ability to see, speak, hear, and feel. It was a formula that ran counter to Plato's concept of autonomous self "symbolized as the power to think, to calculate, to cogitate, and to know" (206).

Certain inferences can be drawn from Ong's and Havelock's theories. The first is that the appearance of writing in these cultures resulted in, or at least was instrumental in, the alienation of the spoken word. It was no longer tied to acoustic production by voice. It could be objectified and made visible instead of being evanescent. By that act, writing aided the abstraction of not only language but also human thought, separating it from the imagism that characterized its oral existence.

The second point is that oral narratives were not regarded as flights of fancy but as a body of the community's cultural and philosophical thoughts, even as the actual performance of these narratives was equally aesthetically and emotionally pleasing. Thus, the narratives were rigorously composed and kept alive in the consciousness of the citizenry through memorization and ability to recall, as well as through performances to the accompaniment of music. Equally significant, verbal performance was intrinsically associated with superior cognitive abilities. Ruth Finnegan's study of the interfaces between orality and literacy among the Limba people of Sierra Leone in West Africa is particularly relevant. According to Finnegan, despite the concrete presence of literacy among the Limba, the mark of intelligence and of authority is located in speech, signified by the term *bafunuŋ*. "Speaking" validated social contracts in the very way that written documents function in most literacy-dominant societies. With regard to the construction of abstract thought, Finnegan writes:

> If you ask a Limba the meaning of *bafunuŋ* (a wise/clever/intelligent man) the explanation is almost always in terms of his capacity to *speak*. . . .
> [I]n Limba language the particular noun class which refers to words to do with language is the same as the class containing abstract nouns. The possibility of abstract terms and abstract thought is, for the Limba, directly associated with speech—rather than, as often with us [the West?], with writing or perhaps inner thoughts. (58)

With this clear evidence of orality as the preferred mode of demonstrating high cognitive ability, it is difficult to agree with Jack Goody's claims that "cognitively as well as sociologically, writing underpins 'civilization,' the culture of cities" (300).[13]

Plato's banishment of affective poetry from the polis stemmed from the development of a new concept that valorized the thinking being outside of his/her psychosomatic and physiological referents. The alienation of the performer from the audience that takes place in writing made it possible to forge new modes of thought that unwittingly gave the impression that the Homeric age, because of the primacy of the spoken word, was not capable of the sophisticated ordering and reordering of words and ideas that writing immediately made possible.

Recent scholarship, however, has revealed the complexity of oral performance. The systemic arrangement of thoughts in definite patterns and their articulation through several oral rhetorical strategies demonstrate an active consciousness. Ong calls these strategies the "psychodynamics of orality" (*Orality and Literacy* 30). They include the formulaic styling of thought and experience, a mnemonically preserved lore of the land, a rhetorical formula of addition and repetition that enables the performer to maintain communicative equilibrium with the audience and perhaps, most importantly, the emphatic and participatory nature of spoken performance.

A discussion of orality and literacy cannot be altogether effective if critical attention is consistently placed on their dissimilarities, the features that, as Finnegan puts it, constitute the "Great Divide" (12ff). Yet these dissimilarities need attention. The differences are most evident when comparing writing to the operational dynamics of an oral narrative performance. By performance, I refer to Richard Bauman's view that it is

> a mode of communication, a way of speaking, the essence of which resides in the assumption of responsibility to an audience for a display of communicative skill, highlighting the way in which communication is carried out, above and beyond its referential content. From the point of view of the audience, the act of expression on the part of the performer is thus laid open to evaluation for the way it is done, for the relative skill and effectiveness of the performer's display. (*Story, Performance, and Event* 3)

Bauman's definition establishes a framework for our understanding of the oral performance. The performer has a responsibility to his or her audience and wins their critical attention through the display of skills that appeal to their senses. It is not static; it is not merely the narrated event but the event of narration that is called into account in this mutual oneness of audience with artist that Ropo Sekoni refers to as "aesthetic transaction" (10). The open-endedness of the performance moment makes it a "living process by which performance is continually actualized" (Okpewho, *Epic* 50).

Conversely, in the written medium, the word, which in oral performance is received as an extension of the performer, slumps lifeless onto paper (as contrived letters). As an individual and isolated exercise, the narrative event in a written mode grapples with new strategies that are aimed at restoring the severed "aesthetic transaction." The writer's attempt to attain a successful performance similar to an oral one results in a different schematization of the narrative. I would like to suggest that the penetration of characters in written narratives, for instance, is a feature meant to complement the vivid portrayal and dramatization of characters in an oral performance. This point will be explored in detail while discussing Jean Toomer's *Cane* in chapter 5.

Even though some of the scholars whose works I have referenced do not apply exclusively to African or Afro-diasporic narratives, the issues they raise are germane to the question of orality and literacy in the Afro-diasporic literary tradition. For one, the existence in Africa of traditional art forms that are largely oral and of modern literary forms that are sustained by a literate culture offers a good opportunity for analyzing and discussing the relation between the spoken and the written word in Afro-diasporic literature. One way of explaining the relationship is through the impact of the two main epochs of Africa's contact with Europe, namely, slavery and colonization. Although before contact with the West, some African civilizations had developed alphabets and such other indices of literacy, what today goes as written African literature is largely a consequence of encounters with the Islamic and European world. That these encounters have influenced the nature and meaning of African literature, there is no doubt; what remains debatable is the extent of the influence of the colonial/Western encounter in the study of contemporary Afro-diasporic literature.

The New World experience of the encounter is particularly remarkable. In the United States, the African slaves were by default inscribed into the literate culture of the dominant Anglo-European Americans. The slave master's use of the Bible as a pacifying agent further exposed the Africans to the structured and formalized world of the written word (even though the formal education of the African was seriously discouraged). Despite this exposure, the core of African American literature is located in the folkloric tradition. In *Talkin and Testifyin*, Geneva Smitherman not only demonstrates how oral verbal skill is the hallmark of African American speech but also shows how this characteristic is directly related to an African worldview. Hence she states, "The persistence of the African-based oral tradition is such that blacks tend to place only limited value on the written word, whereas verbal skills expressed orally rank in high esteem" (76). Smitherman then identifies the various verbal forms in black vernacular, which include the call-and-response performance of the traditional black church sermon, rap, signifyin', and the dozens.

On the other hand, the African slaves in the Caribbean, who occupied a hostile cultural space where the use of their native languages was strongly discouraged, evolved new modes of cultural expression. Kamau E. Brathwaite, the celebrated Barbadian poet, identifies the evolution of an alternative mode of expression as borne primarily through what he calls

"Nation Language" (*History of the Voice* 13). Forced to learn a European language, the Africans nonetheless subjected the alien tongue to their needs, creating Nation Language, which, Brathwaite indicates, "is influenced very strongly by the African model, the African aspect of our New World/ Caribbean heritage" (13). It is an oral-based linguistic medium that incorporates the verbal nuances of their African ancestry and, in contemporary times, has influenced the character of African Caribbean art—poetry, music, the novel, and other expressive forms. Indeed, in calling for the extension of the frontiers of its usage, Brathwaite sees Nation Language as a liberatory tool capable of steering Caribbean literature from European models to a new homegrown paradigm (49).

What blacks in Africa, the Americas, and Europe point to through their distinct literary heritage and their checkered experience in global history is the necessity of recognizing a paradigm that does not conform to any erroneously totalizing model of art but rather represents the set of values that inform black people's appreciation or rejection of works of art by their artists. The call for the formulation of an Afro-diasporic literary aesthetic based on the recognition of the oral-written interplay in texts forms the foundation of the following exploration.

In *Caribbean Poetics*, Silvio Torres-Saillant observes that among Caribbean writers there is a "historical imagination" that accounts for their interest in creating works that reexamine the history of the region (90). Torres-Saillant notes that the conviction that the history of the Caribbean has been written mostly by Western colonialists and West Indians sympathetic to the West "breeds a widespread desire to undertake a general historiographical repair in the area" among Caribbean artists (91). The existence of various racial and ethnic groups in the region, all with their unique historical experiences and encounters with the West, further propels the need to reexamine or—to use Torres-Saillant's word—"repair" the dominant narratives that tend to erase those differences. By reconstructing the past in ways that are meaningful to the Caribbean experience, the writers implicitly engage in a conversation on the conceptualization of a Caribbean Voice. When writers such as Wilson Harris, Roy Heath, and Alejo Carpentier deploy mythohistorical strategies in their narratives, they point to the link between the idioms of narration and the narratives they constitute. Thus, the narrative forms operate within a Caribbean worldview that destabilizes Western constructions of history and narrative.

Folklore not only occupies a unique position in addressing the connection between the oral and the written, but it is also the central constituent in the African diasporic narrative tradition. From myths to the dozens, from the trickster to the black sermon traditions, an aesthetic based on the dynamics of folk expression can be discerned. An expressive tradition fashioned from the interaction of the community at the grass roots not only forms the foundation of much of African and Afro-diasporic art, but it also constitutes the paradigm by which it may be appreciated. The business of appreciation needs to be highlighted, as it significantly bears on this study.

Textual Specifics

This study is premised on according due recognition to the artistic integrity of blacks in the diaspora, even when tracing the African "genealogy of culture and cultural expression" among writings of persons of African descent in the New World is implicated (John 8). For a while, tracing African roots in the artistic creations of blacks in the New World has tended to generate much attention, as if to suggest that the New World does not have a profound impact on their creative spirit.[14] It is only in his formulation of a separate space for the African diaspora that I find Gilroy's intervention useful, especially as I have deliberately chosen only black writers from the Americas for study. Other aspects of Gilroy's position are problematic, especially where they have sought to undermine the integrity of black/African cultural consciousness or dismissed the legitimacy and relevance of African roots for African diasporic discourse.

I have selected four authors for this study. Roy A. K. Heath and Wilson Harris are from Guyana, while Toni Morrison and Jean Toomer are from the United States. By choosing Heath and Harris, I do not mean to cast them as representatives of the Caribbean writers, nor do I intend such for Morrison and Toomer. I selected Harris and Heath for their consistency in representing the mythic consciousness of their native cultural and geographical space in their narratives, even though both writers reside in the United Kingdom. On the other hand, I have chosen Morrison for her consistent engagement with the representation of African American experience, through her performance and interrogation of the uses of folklore and the oral tradition in her novels. Toomer's *Cane* serves as a model for understanding the process of transposing oral folklore to print. It is equally a viable text for the application of oral performative criticism.

Chapter 2 examines Heath's representation of the Guyanese mythic figures, Old Higue, Durga, and Bakoo, in his novels. My reason is that Heath's application of folklore is not for embellishment; rather, an understanding of the Guyanese mythic figures, especially those that feature in what Heath calls the "anxiety-lore" of the land, is crucial for grasping meaning in his novels.

Harris's reconceptualization of literacy in light of the oral imagination is central to the texts examined in chapter 3. He subverts the notion by resting it on the ability not to read and write but to perceive or imagine reality from the mundane and the sublime. Offered as a counterdiscourse to rigid Western constructs of reality, Harris argues that the oral mind, with its ability to traverse the material world, its limitless space, and its capacity for adapting to constantly changing ideologies and ontologies, is the inheritor of the form of literacy that Harris calls the "literacy of the imagination." This notion, I suggest, is significant, for it changes the power equation between the binary and hierarchized reasoning of Western civilization and other civilizations that privilege the type of perception Harris explores. I have selected the later works of Harris, not only because they offer a fresh portal into Harris's lifetime artistic and political preoccupation but also because of my interest in contributing to scholarship on these texts, which, as opposed to the earlier ones, have received considerably less attention. Invariably, I would argue that it would not be too difficult to apply some of my conclusions here to the earlier works. It is in that light that the chapter devotes some space to considering Harris's first novel, *The Palace of the Peacock.*

Chapter 4 is devoted to three novels by Toni Morrison and continues the exploration of the place of memory in narrative. I examine the implications of the oral imagination on history and community. From *Song of Solomon,* which shows the power of communal memory to counter a hegemonic history; to *Paradise,* where this memory and its narrative performance are subverted; to *Jazz,* which features a collage of contestatory narrative perspectives, Morrison interrogates the idea of a neutral oral tradition that always serves the needs of the oppressed, especially as it relates to African American experience. What my study reveals is a folkloric presence in Morrison's novels that is both celebratory and interrogative.

In the final chapter, "'Singing Before the Sun Goes Down': Jean Toomer's *Cane* and the Black Oral Performance Aesthetic," I offer a performative reading of *Cane.* Critics have failed to pay adequate attention to the text's oral performance background. While some note folkloric materials in the text, a study of how the different creative acts in it cohere to form a single performance is rarely done. This chapter redresses this absence by presenting black oral performance aesthetic as the interpretive tool for reading *Cane.* By this gesture, *Cane* becomes a quintessential model showing the positive transformation that occurs when the black oral tradition speaks in the written medium.

This book proposes an interpretive model for the reading of the Afro-diasporic novel that pays attention to folklore not as an ingredient in the narratives but as the basis for the narratives. The works I have analyzed here do not contain folklore materials; they *are* folklore, constituted by the intersections of oral narrative aesthetics, New World sensibility, and the written tradition. As I have stated earlier, the study seeks to expand our understanding of the forms of folklore as it pertains to black texts. The book seeks to demonstrate the durability of the black aesthetic as formed in the spoken word and made manifest in the written.

− TWO −

Roy A. K. Heath and Guyanese Anxiety Lore

Give us a few hundred years and we will be a nation of *douglas,* mixed Indians and Creoles, with dim memories of our ancestral homes in Africa and India, the alpha and omega of man's destiny. At the end, with the marriage of Shango and Durga, will not our mutual resentments be washed away in the torrential rains of history?

—Roy A. K. Heath, *The Ministry of Hope*

In many of Roy Heath's novels, the representation of the mythic imagination drawn from folklore is not cosmetic. Rather, it interrogates Caribbean reality, revisiting the Caribbean past through the mythic sign and, most importantly, fashioning a unique aesthetic paradigm that takes into consideration both its Guyanese and African heritage. There is, of course, the problem of defining "reality," or realism, in either myth or in the novelistic tradition. E. M. Forster's casual but basic statement in *Aspects of the Novel* that the novel "tells a story" (45, 68) may be adequate in helping locate the commonality of both forms as narrative. But it does not help in distinguishing what form this narrative takes and what claims it makes to "factuality." For while Isidore Okpewho would regard myth as "that quality of fancy which informs the creative or configurative powers of the human mind in varying degrees of intensity" (*Myth* 69), the insistent claims of the modern novel to be seen as a faithful representation of daily life seem to put it at opposite ends from the qualitatively higher license with which myth represents existence.[1] In *The Rise of the Novel,* Ian Watt argues that the most distinguishing mark of the novel is its "formal realism" by which it presents "a full and authentic report of human experience," conveyed "through a more largely referential use of language" (32). Watt concedes that this verisimilitudinal feature is not unique to the eighteenth-century novel, considering that Homer used it in his epic songs, and some later artists employed it as well, though he adds that the difference is that they did not pursue the device "wholeheartedly" (33).

If Watt is constrained to rank the referential use of language by degrees of the artist's devotion or otherwise to the strategy, it may be that the problem lies in defining what "human experience" is and, related to this, the capacity of the novel, as he has identified it, to represent that experience. The issue of what constitutes human experience is an ontological one, for it concerns a society's sense of being and its relation to the world. Invariably, an ontological viewpoint dictates the reality a narrative represents.

In her study of Wilson Harris, Alejo Carpentier, and Edouard Glissant, Barbara Webb shows how the novels of the three Caribbean writers "assume the role of myth as historical memory and speculative inquiry intended to provoke consciousness" (6). Webb's study reveals that myth is the viable means of representing reality by the Caribbean writer. Her statement further suggests the idea of myth as both a historical ("factual") entity and a speculative (imaginary) construct.[2] In any case, for the African Caribbean, the mythic aesthetic is cogent. Not only is it effective in representing their world picture; it also creates an aesthetic category that helps in the appreciation and understanding of African Caribbean literature.

For good reasons, the African Caribbean's return to African aesthetics is significant. Reality in African ontology exists through a nebulous interaction between realms of perception. Indeed, rather than creating a distinction between fantasy and the temporal, the African idea of reality, as Wole Soyinka suggests in his work on the African ritual archetype, is one borne through the archetypal hero's withdrawal "into an inner world from which he returns communicating a new strength for action." To make a profound statement of difference between this experience and the European model, Soyinka posits: "The definition of this inner world as 'fantasy' betrays a Eurocentric conditioning or alienation." He further explains that such a withdrawal by the human agent is not a transition from a conscious reality, per se, to a trance but "rather that his consciousness is stretched to embrace another and primal reality" (Myth 33).

Soyinka's argument is important, considering the place of folklore, or myth in particular, in African narratives. It expands the experiential perception captured through the novel and equally demands a distinct way of seeing, of understanding and interpreting this stretch from the temporal to primordial reality. Wilson Harris's theory of "alchemy" addresses this need. In *The Womb of Space*, Harris engages the multicultural and historical consciousness of the African Caribbean, arguing that such consciousness can only be represented through an artistic module that "subsists on *evolution and alchemy* [and] acquires a concreteness of vision in its multipigmented arc that runs deeper and wider than the scope of realism that seems both naturally fated and blind to the mystery of reality" (71). Harris's "mystery of reality," like Soyinka's "hinterland of transition," supplants Watt's brand of the English novel that seems to approach the genre through a mechanistic polarization of what is reality and what is not. To Soyinka, the African process of appropriating what is not temporally perceived as part of material existence runs counter to the "Western cast of mind, a compartmentalizing habit of thought which periodically selects aspects of human emotion, phenomenal observations . . . and turns them into separatist myths" (*Myth* 37). Realism to the African Caribbean is both material and transcendent. From the "ordinariness" of everyday existence to the scars of a traumatic historical experience, the community weaves narratives that validate and give life to that existence, as well as establish themselves as the totem for group identity and destiny.

Myth and Folklore as Narrative Signs

In a short essay, "The Function of Myth," in which he examines folklore in Guyana, Heath describes Guyanese myths as "the evidence of the life-force of our nation" (91). They are narratives embodying varying personalities and traits, made remarkable by their strangeness even though their presence and activities are observable in daily life.

There is Old Higue, a witch who sheds her skin by night and hides it under a mortar. She then travels as a ball of fire to the home of her victim, usually a child, and sucks the child's blood. A sure sign of Old Higue's visitation is a stiff neck on waking up, or a high fever, and in some cases, death. Mothers try to protect their young ones from Old Higue by hanging amulets around their neck and waists. Old Higue is similar to the Hindus' Durga, the devourer of children. Crying children cut off their tantrums on threats to summon Durga. Another lore figure is White Lady, the tall, blue-eyed woman known for the iciness of her touch and her penchant for killing young children.

Bakoo is another figure in Guyanese lore. He is a little man kept in a bottle. When fed milk and banana at regular intervals and released on moonless nights, he brings fortune to his owner. But when he breaks loose on being denied his staple, he wreaks havoc, damaging property. Bakoo's existence poses enormous challenges to the owner for the simple reason that a breach of the fixed mealtimes endangers both the owner's life and property. Yet he is a sign of sure wealth, even though the overabundance of the wealth Bakoo bestows on his beneficiary is bound to create a rift between the person and their neighbors. There are other figures in the Guyanese oral tradition that Heath mentions, but the ones described above will suffice for the present discussion.

In the conclusion of his essay, Heath declares: "It is to our creative artists, our writers, painters, sculptors and musicians that we must look to rebuild a shattered tradition [i.e. the folkloric tradition], intended to serve the aspirations of the Guyanese *as a whole*" (91; original emphasis). The year after the publication of this essay (1974), Heath matched his own challenge with the publication of his first novel, *A Man Come Home,* a work centered on Fairmaid ("Water Mama"), princess of the rivers. In exchange for an undivided loyalty from her mortal male lover, Fairmaid blesses the lover with riches. This and other mythic figures drawn from Guyanese lore constitute the core of Heath's narrative schemata. Identifying the role and presence of these figures is very important in understanding some of the dominant motifs in Heath's art, such as the overriding sense of doom, the preponderant use of dreams as extensions of reality, and the use of the mask idiom.

In his analysis of the portrayal of female characters in Heath's novels, Mark A. McWatt notes that one of the issues raised in Heath's novels is the "sense in which characters are victimized by the author himself, by his deliberate choice of a particular mode of writing" (223). McWatt identifies this mode as tragic irony. The seemingly pervasive sense of gloom that encircles the world of his novels even as the novelist portrays ordinary characters seeking ordinary goals, argues McWatt, "can often create a sense of deformity . . . a sense that the situations and events described do not ring quite true or seem somehow unreal—as do all effects that have been cut off from their causes" (224). While it is rather strange to charge a storyteller with victimizing his or her characters (as if they could be anything but what the creator wants them to be!), what McWatt labels tragic irony cannot sufficiently explain the symbolism that many of the characters embody. There is deliberateness in the process by which meaning is generated through character representation in Heath's novels, so that what appears to be a "deformity" or victimization may be understood as operating within a complex but carefully laid-out structure. This structure we can understand in a broad context as the folkloric aesthetic fashioned to transmit meaning.

The events that McWatt reads as untrue or unreal can be explained by noting how Heath uses folklore for characterization and narrative. In this kind of storytelling, the case cannot be made that the situations or characters one encounters in Heath's novels are unreal or improbable as McWatt charges. The presence of myth in his narrative precludes any attempt to read the texts through a limited view of realism; structured as novels, Heath's narratives still distinguish themselves as products of a mythic configuration. Events and characters unfold inexorably along pre-ordained folkloric resolution. By the success of this effort, Heath seems to be vindicating Gregory L. Lucente's positional statement in *The Narrative of Realism and Myth* about mythic and realist discourse as both representing fictional modes, only that "[i]n narrative fiction, the transcendent fullness of myth, which locates its significance not in the world of time and matter, but in a realm beyond temporal and spatial limitation, thus complements the worldly plenitude of the realist sign, as it recodes on an idealized level what realist representation codes on the material one" (40). I have not used the word "borrow" in describing Heath's deployment of the folkloric resources available to him in most of his novels since it does not seem to me that the connection is that of dependence. Instead, Heath's narratology and mode of perception operate *within* the oral mythic aesthetic of his Guyanese milieu.

Here it is important to note the pioneering effort of Amon Saba Saakana in his work *Colonization and the Destruction of the Mind: Psychosocial Issues of Race, Class, Religion and Sexuality in the Novels of Roy Heath*. There Saakana rightly argues against the continued application of Euro-American theoretical paradigms in the study of African Caribbean texts. Saakana's work gives insight into the articulation of a Caribbean literary paradigm, and his discussion on the dynamics of myth in Caribbean narratives is especially worth noting. On the capacity of myth to be responsive to the artistic imagination, he states: "Mythology is not static. It does not remain suspended in history or in the air. It comes alive when writers begin to reinterpret and utilize its symbols to inform us of the present or of the past; only then its relevance takes on special meaning and impact" (42). This is certainly true when applied to the works of Heath or his fellow citizen, Wilson Harris. However, the concerns of Saakana in *Colonization and the Destruction of the Mind* and the conclusions he draws in his reading of some of Heath's novels are different from my present concerns.

Saakana's work adequately addresses issues of orality, literacy, and colonialism and their impact on gender relations and economic and social well-being in the novels of Heath. My interest, however, is on the mythic imagination in Roy Heath's three novels, with emphasis on the aesthetic ideology that informs the writer's imagination. One instance of difference in our interest could be seen in his analysis of Galton Flood, the protagonist in *The Murderer*. At the end of the novel, Galton suffers what appears to be a mental breakdown. Saakana argues that the Guyanese society is responsible for Galton's fate (86). I would rather suggest that Galton's state of consciousness operates within a concept I call "embottlement": the idea of potentiality inherent in the African Guyanese myth of Bakoo, the tiny man in a bottle. Galton is a restless character who is unable to maintain an emotionally stable relationship with his wife because he feels trapped in a marriage that constricts his well-being. I would suggest that his final mental condition indicates his freedom, albeit with the risks associated with a released Bakoo. Sakaana's reading is informed by a materialist ideology that looks at the economic and social forces that impinge on the character; however, understanding the mythic tradition from which Galton's character emerges yields a more complex profile of both the character and the novel. The latter conclusion, I think, warrants the view that Saakana's work has limited value in unlocking meaning in some of Heath's novels.

Durga/Old Higue and Matriarchal Dominance

The strong influence that mothers in Heath's novels have over their children, especially their male offspring, is a "realist" transformation of such female folkloric figures as Old Higue, Durga, Water Mama, and White Lady. In *The Shadow Bride*, Heath's eighth novel, Mrs. Singh's possessiveness looms over her entire household. Mrs. Singh, an Indian widow of a former indentured laborer, attempts to chart a new life for herself and the large household she rules, but she runs into conflict with her only son, Betta, a medical doctor. Against her late husband's plan that Betta be sent to a public school, possibly to expose the boy to the multiethnic Guyanese society, Mrs. Singh instead contracts the education of her son to Mulvi Sahib, a Muslim cleric. She chooses private tuition for Betta as a way of distinguishing herself from her neighbors because, as she puts it, "she had not come to the country as an indentured labourer and had no intention of suffering either directly or vicariously the humiliations heaped on the children of estate workers" (6).

Mrs. Singh's determination to maintain ethnic purity in a country of multiple cultures stems from her spite for the East Indian's social class in the highly stratified Guyanese society. Having been brought to the Caribbean as indentured servants, the East Indians are not respected by either the black or the Amerindian population. Worse, those in the immigrant group were also insignificant back on the old continent, despite their air of superiority over the other groups. Mrs. Singh had married her Indian-born husband who had "dazzled her family with jewellery and his knowledge of foreign parts," but he had "turned out to be a nobody in the country from which he came" (7). At his death, Mrs. Singh decides not to let her only son end up as insignificant as his father does. Betta's eventual return from abroad as a qualified medical doctor raises her esteem in the East Indian community where she has grown to be regarded as a powerful but very magnanimous figure whose word is accepted without question.

Unfortunately, for Mrs. Singh, her decision to give Betta an elitist and prestigious education also turns out to be the source of conflict and final estrangement from him. Betta returns from England to rediscover the abject life of the poor East Indian working in the sugarcane estates and decides to work as a medical officer in one of the remote estates. His mother resists his plans, having intended that her son assume prominence in the East Indian community in Georgetown. Her scorn for the East Indian laborers also underscores her opposition to Betta's decision, as she sees them as bereft of industry and sense of achievement. To aggravate her disappointment further, Betta shows no particular interest in choosing his acquaintances from the East Indian community and cultivates a close friendship with Neil Merriman, a Creole pharmacist.

The Shadow Bride is Heath's most extensive novel yet and resembles in terms of its broad time frame and thematic occupation V. S. Naipaul's A House for Mister Biswas. Both novels deal with several generations of an East Indian family ruled by powerful matriarchal figures who struggle without success to retain their original Indian ways in the plural West Indian society. Both novels chart a tragic course for their heroines: their marked despair upon witnessing the inexorable crumbling of cherished values dictated by the sharp contrast of their native lands to the postplantation New World reality. But what distinguishes Heath's novel from Naipaul's, or from works by Samuel Selvon on the same subject, is Heath's success in representing this contemporary theme in the realm of the mythic. He presents the conflict between Mrs. Singh and Betta as a mortal battle between Durga and a harassed but resilient "victim."

The birth of Betta occurs after five miscarriages. Though Aji, the old female member of the household, claims the stillbirths were a result of malaria, the narrator leaves enough suggestions that Durga is implicated in the deaths. First, the Pujaree, a bogus Hindu priest who succeeds in displacing the Muslim teacher Mulvi Sahib in Mrs. Singh's confidence, schemes to have her prostrate before Durga's image in his temple, "the self-same Durga who had robbed her of her children" (44). At the end, she is more than a devotee; in fact, one might argue that she becomes the embodiment of Durga. Rather than be repelled by Durga's hand in her childbirth misfortunes, Mrs. Singh privately attaches herself to lore figures with Old Higue's and Durga's attributes: "She could confide in no one how she identified herself with the heroines of destructive myths, who ate their children or slaughtered, for no other reason than an obsessive jealousy which did not grow tepid with the passing months, but rather thrived, attained an autonomy, then took to the subterranean caverns of her thoughts" (98). It is clear that even if the narrator does not directly identify Mrs. Singh as Durga, her character, as gleaned from this internal monologue, closely aligns with the lore figure. What the narrator describes as an autonomous destructive thought simmering at the subconscious level of the "shadow bride" can reasonably be regarded as "possession."[3] Better still, to go back to Soyinka's ritual grammar, Mrs. Singh's thoughts are the articulation of her primordial or mythic reality. Thus, her seeming concern for members of her household and her show of generosity to the poor are not genuine but rather destructive, as deleterious as the blood-sucking activities of Old Higue.

The reader's first consciousness of Mrs. Singh as the avatar of Durga comes alive through one of Betta's childhood recollections. Thinking over his mother's voracious effort to control his medical practice, Betta remembers how

> As a small boy he used to associate her with the colour blue, after an illuminated print of Durga in her benevolent aspect. Then, one night . . . he dreamt of her with staring eyes and a long tongue which hung over her lower lip. And soon afterwards, among the numerous old calendars she kept in her camphor-wood chest, he discovered a picture of Durga in her terrible aspect, the devourer of children. The picture was red and baleful. And what remained of the experience, what lingered until his childhood was overtaken by his youth, was the ascendancy of red over blue. (57–58)

These images do not exist in the novel as the fantasies of a child. They pursue Betta throughout his fight with his mother. She discreetly works with the Pujaree to bewitch Betta in order to coerce a favor from him and nearly strangles Meena, Betta's wife. It is significant that the realization of the malevolent personality of his mother occurs at night and in a dream state. The discovery of his mother's association with Durga is set in a dream, and the malevolent aspects of Durga become the ingredients that fuel the antagonism between mother and son.

Furthermore, the transformation of Mrs. Singh's color from benign blue to ravishing red foregrounds the seeming beneficence in Mrs. Singh's desiring that Rani, one of her maids, having married, continue to live in her mansion with her husband. The "goodwill" turns out to be dubious. When Betta rebels against her influence by choosing to work in the estate, she decides to take her revenge on him by scheming to hurt Rani, whom Betta loves. Rani, aware of Mrs. Singh's "destructive impulse" (95–96), wants to leave the mansion with her husband, Tipu, so that they can live independently. However, taking advantage of Tipu's indolence, Mrs. Singh is able to bring him completely under her influence, thus effectively retaining the couple in her prison. The image of Mrs. Singh as Old Higue comes through as Rani prepares to give birth and the narrator shows Mrs. Singh's Durgan pleasure over the impending birth and the extention of her dominance thus: "She had decided that that influence must also extend to the child when it was born, over its education and its comings and goings. And Rani would be obliged to yield to the opportunities afforded her offspring *as one succumbed to the influence of a debilitating drug that seduced before it destroyed*" (99; emphasis added).

Mrs. Singh's plan to destroy the mother of a baby in order to own the unborn child parallels Old Higue's terrifying preying on the life force of children. The mythic transference reaches its full manifestation when Mrs. Singh, working in concert with the Pujaree, casts a spell over Betta and tries to cajole him into agreeing to hand over his child to be raised under their ultraconservative Hindu lifestyle. By the spell (Betta rather believes that she drugged him) she leads Betta to a room where she pleads with desperate urgency, "If you give me your son I'd do anything . . . I'd move out of the house and leave it for you and your family" (350). Mrs. Singh's life depends on this child, just as Old Higue depends on the children's blood for her survival. Mrs. Singh makes her dependence more poignant when she leads Betta to another room where two boys and three girls are playing. She tells Betta, "They are your brothers and sisters, my aborted children, driftwood, bobbing up and down on the sea; but put your hands to catch them and they vanish" (350). It seems this surreal evocation of the dead children deepens Mrs. Singh's sense of loss. However, the point that the children are in a room under Mrs. Singh's control leaves the impression that they are her prisoners, her victims, the ones whose blood she needs to stay alive. When Arjun is later born with a disability, it confirms the potency of the Obeah she wrought with the Pujaree to harm the child prior to the child's birth (357).

Despite Mrs. Singh's destructive impulses and the fear she conjures in everyone around her, Heath rests the moral strength of the narrative on Betta and his wife Meena, their children, the Merrimans, and the other characters that see Guyana as their homeland even when they recognize difference in their racial origins. Mrs. Singh's influence and power self-destruct; she kills herself after a final effort to kill Meena, possess Arjun, and reestablish control over Betta. What the novel thus seems to suggest is that a narcissist desire to turn the Guyanese world into the Old one is fatally destructive, in fact, as threatening as the spell of Durga or Old Higue.

Bakoo and Psychic Potentiality

The myth of Bakoo, the tiny man corked inside a bottle, assumes an equally prominent position in Heath's writing. In his state of imprisonment, Bakoo has the potential of wreaking havoc if he manages to escape from the bottle. On the other hand, if properly taken care of and released at certain times, Bakoo brings fortune to his owner. Thus, for the Guyanese, as Heath rightly concludes, "he is the lore-figure of property and ambition" ("Function of Myth" 87). The intriguing feature of this myth is the idea of *potentiality*. The dividing line between destructive ambition and a constructive one is merged into a symmetry of meaning so that the state of bottle encystment becomes a vortex as fraught with possibilities as Ogun's descent to the "chthonian realm."[4]

The Bakoo myth, like Old Higue's, characterizes what Heath refers to as the "anxiety-lore" of the African Guyanese. These stories expose the frustration of the African slaves in both their relationship with their masters and their physical environment. Like the tiny man, their owners exploited them to generate wealth and gave them just enough food to keep them alive. More important, it signifies the bottled potential of the Africans seeking release.

The Bakoo idiom conveys the apparently nihilistic portrait of many of Heath's major characters. Rather than engaging the paradoxical aspect of the traditional Bakoo narrative, Heath's Bakoo hardly escapes from the bottle. Unlike the myth of Ogun, the Yoruba god of creativity and destruction who descends into the chthonian realm and emerges with a potent liberatory force, Heath's narratives explore the Bakoo myth from the point of the enclosure. The conflicts and struggles that take place within the bottle take center stage in these stories—a phenomenon I identified earlier as embottlement. The effect is a presentation of characters whose existence seems to be impinged upon by forces beyond them and shaped by their recognition of being trapped inside without hope of release.

Heath interprets Bakoo's embottlement as that unknown quantity that is always elusive to the inquirer and thus a potential source of frustration. Such an interpretation also illuminates Galton Flood's character in *The Murderer*. Set in the early 1920s, *The Murderer* focuses on Galton Flood, his unease in a world of struggle, his marriage to Gemma, and his eventual murder of his wife as he is caught in a vortex of marital bewilderment. Part of his dilemma is the struggle to break out of an emotional prison imposed on him by an imperious and castrating mother. At the age of ten he has been completely emasculated by his mother, who regards him as having a "weak constitution," and when a female schoolmate comes calling at Galton's house, he is so totally intimidated by the mockery of his mother that he keeps inside, "his eyes closed tight in shame" (9).

Not only is Galton incapable of entering into a normal relationship with a woman, but the result of the abuse inflicted by his mother also inculcates in him a warped sense of purity. Raised by a mother determined to instill in him a loathing for his father and invariably a fear of her authority and sexuality, Galton's "weak constitution" fosters an exaggerated notion of sin. In one incident, Galton pays a social visit to his friend, the Walk-Man, and finds out that like his late father, the Walk-Man also dreads his wife, whom the Walk-Man describes as a "battleaxe" (25). Significantly, Galton literally experiences fits on his first sighting of the Walk-Man's wife as she immediately evokes in his harassed mind the image of his late mother. Galton's reaction exposes his sense of emotional entrapment that even the death of his mother cannot wipe out, a nihilistic censorship that diminishes his capacity to love, to seek pleasure. Consequently, Galton interprets such emotions as dangerous and transgressive: "He felt certain that the fright he received earlier on, on catching sight of her, was connected with the self-indulgence of his life at Wismar. His guilt at the pleasure he found in Gemma's company, never far from the surface, had taken the form of the woman's fancied resemblance to his mother" (27). Galton's self-denial stems from this guilt, a complex that also requires his guarding his scuttled emotions jealously. His discovery that Gemma is not a virgin on their first night as a married couple shatters his fragile sense of love as he feels soiled by her transgression.

Moreover, Galton's abhorrence of premarital sex is not mere prudishness. It stems from an obsession with the mapping of and strict adherence to boundaries. The narrator notes that the reason Galton has not "soiled his body in pre-marital association" is not so much because of the guilt it will cause him as its potential to render him "incapable of exercising that moral authority he associated with the head of a family" (56–57). His expectations of a wife, his perceived obligations as a husband, and the separation of his inner anxieties from the responsibilities of maintaining a relationship with his marital, consanguine, and social relationships are intertwined with what the narrator describes as his obsession with "the boundaries of propriety, of pride, of privacy, of love" (58). For Galton, Gemma's infidelity marks a breach of propriety, a hurt to his pride, but, more importantly, a cause for regret for exposing himself to be soiled after venturing outside the protective cyst of his emotional solitude. It is a loss of an intangible inner bearing that also marks the beginning of an inexorable decline in his capacity to be at home with himself and the world around him. The planning and execution of Gemma's murder is done without much emotion except that in killing her, he lets loose a repressed anger seething inside him from an abused childhood (109).

Consequently, Gemma's murder operates as a cleansing act, the energizing of a wearied consciousness seeking meaning in a milieu of insipid ambitions and vulgar relationships. Galton feels no sense of grief, no sense of a transgression, no other feeling but plain hunger (110). This illustrates the point Joel Black makes in his book on the aesthetics of murder when he contends: "Considered in the context either of ancient purification rituals or their modern equivalent of aesthetic action, suicide and murder no longer appear merely as transgressions . . . rather, they stand revealed as ecstatic acts of transcendence" (209). On the sheer brutality of the murder, I think that there is a discernible lyricism by which Heath depicts the act. The fluidity of spaces between dream and reality is at the core of the surrealist recreation of the murder scene.[5]

The indignation he feels at the impudence of Gemma to demand his affection dissolves into a dream with an unmitigated realism that captures his inner terror and the frustrations of a jinxed marriage culture: "He had been unwilling to marry because he could not endure a failure as his father had. Now he was so far! Before him lay only ghost-like moon shadows between houses of a deserted road and the eyes behind the lattice-work. He had walked that road a hundred times in his dreams, but only once had found anyone waiting at the end of it: his mother dressed in mauve" (107). The image of his mother appearing at the end of the road powerfully evokes the psychological intimidation she inflicted on him, and apparently, at this moment it is the very personification of his blighted dreams. Perhaps more importantly, Heath swiftly overturns this potentially nightmarish image into a surprising "feeling of elation" as Galton wakes up; what follows is a deliberateness and calmness of purpose as Galton takes Gemma on the fatal trip to the seashore. In addition, a series of anticlimactic incidents follow the murder: Galton suddenly feels hungry and with a good appetite eats a late dinner in a cookshop where some base fellows are entertaining themselves with bawdy jokes that disparage women.

Before proceeding further, I must briefly comment on the matters of gender and sexuality that emerge from Gemma's death. Galton's action, though a reaction to perceived repressed childhood anger, is based on his sexist notion of the woman's place in the home and his desire to control her sexuality. Evidently, Galton regards Gemma as "a being ... whose sexuality exists for someone else who is socially male" (MacKinnon 118). MacKinnon's statement finds expression in Heath's novel in the tense scene of the morning following their wedding night when Galton discovers that Gemma is not a virgin. It does not matter to him that she was a rape victim; instead, he feels dispossessed, robbed of what he considers his prerogative as a husband. Galton experiences a "wave of excitement" as he forces Gemma to recount the rape. His eagerness to hear the story of his wife's traumatic humiliation has the touch of an orgasmic rapture even in his furious anger. Baffled by the intensity of his anger, Gemma asks if the loss of her virginity is *that* important, to which Galton replies, with a slight stammer, "It is important to me. I . . . to me it's the whole basis of our relationship" (75). Centering Gemma's sexuality in his marital relationship is an attempt to recover a childhood where his own sexuality was denied and to possess Gemma's as compensation.

The death of Gemma opens a new pathway in Galton's consciousness. By killing her, Galton stumbles deeply into an abyss of self-annihilation. As he hits the fatal blow on Gemma, he feels "all the repressed anger of his boyhood [come] flooding out like water through a breached koker" (109). Oddly, minutes later, as he tries to unburden his mind to his friend the watchman, he says, "You think I'm grieved. Now it's come to it . . . now I don't even know what I feel" (112).

For Galton there is no tangible release; there is no deliverance from the continued struggle to grasp the thread of his life. Living in limbo, unable to tell the difference between falsehood and truth, between transgression and propriety, he makes a profound statement devoid of pathos: "Life is full of shadows: some of them are soft and others conceal a hammer" (172). The eventual apparent madness of Galton is a consequence, not of guilt for the murder of his wife but of the intensification of a new consciousness that exposes his helplessness at extricating himself from the paradoxical oppression of the female figure as both a purveyor of a castrating sense of self and the very agent of his singed notion of boundaries. Aesthetically, the madness of Galton becomes "a consummation, the ultimate self-expression that is inevitably self-destructive" (Feder xii).

Experiencing a restricted pattern of development and cowed into cultivating a warped sense of manhood and self-worth, Galton ends up with his emotional balance irrevocably shattered. The result is an eccentricity that cannot stand the demands of matrimonial or other interpersonal relationships: he cannot sustain a meaningful relationship with his older brother, Sonny, nor does he make efforts to understand the feelings of his wife. Rather, he becomes restless.

Yet Galton is conscious enough to recognize that he may not be normal any more. He insists that it is not a consequence of killing his wife but "his lack of success at achieving any goal he had set himself and his inability to face up to a situation that had taken him by surprise" (141). The situation in question is Gemma's infidelity. But the credibility of this self-reappraisal is doubtful. It is difficult to identify what he has set as his goals in the first place. There is something abnormal in the agenda of a person who graduates from high school, completes a radio repair course, and chooses to go and work as a watchman in the forest. His frustrations with his family becloud his outlook, and as he tells Winston, his friend from childhood, "life hasn't got dreams, success and all that damn nonsense. Life is full of shadows: some of them are soft and others conceal a hammer. . . . Life itself is a disaster" (172). Evidently, Galton perceives life's hammer more than its softness. The hammer is his failure to cultivate a sociable personality, caused by his own pessimism.

But is it really Galton's pessimism? Heath molds Galton's character around Bakoo. Heath presents an agitated character that evokes the violent struggle of the tiny man in the bottle. Unable to retain his job, haunted by the terrors of his rundown neighborhood, in the following passage Galton's restlessness assumes its ultimate mythic significance: "As Galton walked on, his thoughts became more sombre. Of late he was dogged by the belief that he was in a bottle and was afraid that if he fell asleep someone would come and insert a cork in its mouth, leaving him imprisoned. Once, he even thought he had caught a glimpse of the person waiting in the shadows to catch him asleep" (174). At this point Galton's psyche no longer operates on the tangible plane. His consciousness opens to the world of myth. His obsession with the cork and the bottle, "his frequent cries of 'Don't cork the bottle!'" (189), become his new personality as he slowly passes from the realm of reason to the uncharted world of fantasy.

Bakoo as Trickster Figure

Kwaku, or the Man Who Could Not Keep His Mouth Shut exemplifies yet another dimension of the Bakoo myth in Heath's writing. The novel's folksy narrative style serves as a medium for the delineation of the protagonist Kwaku Cholmondeley's character, a hero who gains notoriety simply by doing nothing. This is what the very first paragraph thematizes: "This is the tale of Kwaku, who was reduced to a state of idiocy by intelligent men, but made a spontaneous recovery. A quick look-around at his fellow men convinced him that there was much protection in idiocy, and that intelligence was like the plimpla palm, bearer of good fruit, but afflicted with thorns. So he fell back into a state of idiocy, only to recover again for love of punishment and a hankering after passion" (7). One may ask, why does the protagonist possess such absurd passions? Kwaku, as the narrator notes, chooses to be an idiot as part of his hankering for the absurd. Unwilling to locate the intelligence of his fellow human beings, he chooses embottlement. Two ideas emerge in this process. First, by opting for a self-imposed idiocy because of a disdain for "intelligence," Kwaku makes a profound statement on the relativity of wit. Significantly, despite his failures and seeming foolery, Kwaku achieves a measure of success by maintaining relative harmony in his large household and commanding the love and respect of his wife, Miss Gwendoline. This degree of success is not too common in Heath's fictive world.

The second is the image of Kwaku as restless Bakoo. The figure of Kwaku as a man who cannot keep his mouth shut is an image drawn from oral tradition.[6] It suggests a passion that is neither within the control of the possessed nor utterly within the bounds of reason. In a surprising swing of fate, very reminiscent of Ganesh's scandalous "success" in V. S. Naipaul's *The Mystic Masseur*, Kwaku becomes a successful healer in New Amsterdam and returns home to a hero's welcome. As he recalls that he had run away from the same village to escape being charged with breaching the village's conservancy, a sudden desire fills his mind as he beams at his appreciative guests: "Had he followed his inclination he would, given his state of mind, almost certainly have admitted to crimes he had not committed, and even invented imaginary crimes, in order to provide his confession with that solid basis which lends to repentance the quality of martyrdom" (150). The consciousness delineated in the preceding statement is not a dim-witted one; Heath creates a character whose notion of reality is a seamless merging of fact and fiction.

What seems like idiocy in the first part of the novel, when Kwaku compulsively volunteers to testify in court as a witness to a car accident he did not witness, turns out in these later scenes to be the product of an active imagination, turning a potentially self-destructive tendency into an agent of creativity. In the court incident, Kwaku participates in the charade with mystifying obstinacy and contradictoriness to the magistrate's consternation (9–12). In another instance, he leaves his family in the village and heads to New Amsterdam in search of employment to help raise their eight children. A stranger to the city, Kwaku is taken in by a couple who forces him to marry their dead teenage daughter. In what is probably the most bizarre event in the novel, Kwaku goes through the arduous rite of trying to slip a ring on the fourth finger of the already decomposing corpse. Days later, he writes a letter to his wife where he tells her his experience. But it is a different story he writes about. The couple who practically held him hostage is now described as "some nice people," and "They had a daughter but she pass away when she was three or four and I had to console them and tell them that death is in the midst of life." Initially, it seems that Kwaku falsifies his harrowing experience to save his family from being overly concerned about his safety and well-being in the city. However, the narrator's comment following the end of the letter suggests otherwise: "Kwaku's lies did not strike him as being odd. Indeed, they were no longer lies, but necessary additions to the dull fare of day-to-day living, like casreep to peeper-pot, or coconut to cook-up rice" (116). Thus, Kwaku is the fabricator of his own reality. In other words, Kwaku recognizes the human thirst for fiction and adventure, and he uses idiocy as a mask for spinning yarns and engaging life in a manner that, in its seeming comicality, actually demonstrates a profound intellect that mocks the idiocy of so-called intelligent persons.

Indeed, the novel is suffused with comedic ebullience that highlights both Kwaku's histrionic actions and the levity with which he sometimes disregards social expectations. He certainly carries the sympathy of the narrator. As shown from the opening paragraph, the narrator's interest is in introducing a quirky character who still manages to attain success despite his seeming determination to fail. He decides at nineteen years old that, "as he had little control of what he said and did, he would get married and so acquire a sense of responsibility," thereby putting the conventional premise for marriage on its head (12). Then he proceeds to draw up a tall order of qualities he wants in a wife, with Blossom his childhood friend his sole point of reference:

> She got to be tall . . . but not too tall. I'd prefer a school teacher, but a dressmaker would do. She musn' get vexed if I come home drunk, but she herself musn't drink. She must know to spell good, but she musn't spend too much time reading. Unless she's a school teacher. She musn't have a flat chest or a huge batty, like Blossom. Blossom man-friend always falling out of bed 'cause she batty does stab him every time he turn. And now he going around with a dislocated arm, all because of she big batty. She must read she Bible and say she prayers . . . She musn't make a noise with she mouth when she eating, like Blossom, who neighbours does know when is lunctime [sic] by the slurping and sucking of the soup in she mouth. . . . Let me see . . . aw . . . le' me see! Oh, yes! She musn't harass me. That's one thing Blossom don' do, harass me. (13)

Kwaku's uncle, who as his guardian has the responsibility of helping him get married, is exasperated by the obduracy of Kwaku's demands but still consents to search for a bride with these qualities. Kwaku's wish list is at once comical and pathetic, revealing his insecurities, but he also displays foresight by desiring a partner with credentials that would make up for his own deficiencies.

The surprising fact is that his uncle does find a woman, Miss Gwendoline, who meets most of Kwaku's criteria—which also includes, "She must respect my friends," prompting his uncle to remind him that he doesn't have any friends (14). Kwaku knows that his uncle cannot wait to absolve himself of the role of being his guardian following the death of his parents, so he exploits his final chance of getting something from his uncle to secure his own economic and social future. In fact, in *The Ministry of Hope*, the sequel to *Kwaku*, Kwaku recalls the incident and surmises, "if his insight deserted him where most things were concerned, there were moments when he displayed a rare understanding of his place in the scheme of things. Did he not lay down the qualifications for any wife his uncle might choose for him, impossible to fulfil if the older man was to be believed? And did he not eventually find Miss Gwendoline, who possessed all the qualities he demanded, and more?" (8). And he achieves this while appearing to be infantile and naïve.

It is the measure of Heath's skills as a great interpreter of the Ananse and Bakoo figures that Kwaku's antics never alienate him from the reader. He is the little man battling powerful forces within and outside and having to rely on his wits to succeed. His methods are effective even if farcical. For example, when his shoemaker employer fires him for taking his photography hobby too seriously, Kwaku quickly realizes the economic damage the job loss would have on his family. But he adopts a roundabout way to beg for restoration. "Right!" he answers back at his employer,

> But don' come round begging me to come back. Right! You know my house, but don' come round. Lot 74C, third house at the back is my direction, but don' come enquiring where K. Cholmondeley live. Don' ask Mr Barzey, who does live in front me uncle, who does live in front of me, because he not going to tell you anything. And although Mr Barzey dog don't bite don' pass his house to come in the back yard looking for me because once I make up my mind, my mind is made up! (42)

You would not think that Kwaku is the one who has just been retrenched. Pretending to be calling the man's bluff, he brazenly gives his employer every bit of contact information that would help the employer locate him should the employer change his mind. Kwaku keeps talking until he strikes the right sentiment in the shoemaker and gets his job back.

The rapid ascent and decline in fortune that Kwaku experiences in his life point to the Bakoo idiom. He is a trickster who builds a successful practice in New Amsterdam by prescribing garlic for almost every conceivable illness. His patients obey his esoteric instructions without questioning, all because "in a fit of inspiration" he had suggested garlic as medicine to a sick man and it apparently worked (118). Nevertheless, his success is always threatened by new vicissitudes. No sooner than Kwaku moves his wife and eight children from their village to the location of his thriving business, his wife mysteriously goes blind, eventually leading to the collapse of his practice. In *Hope*, Kwaku leaves the public service to return to his vocation as healer. As successful as the practice is, Kwaku is overcome by his feelings of inadequacy, precipitated by his very limited formal education. Encouraged and tutored by his son-in-law, he improves his skills in formal English and soon becomes a voracious reader who imports books "for their imposing titles or books that took his fancy only because they were published by a University Press" (182). The unease that Kwaku experiences, in times of both affluence and want, reflects the anxiety inherent in the Bakoo myth. Kwaku represents a successful blending of reality fashioned in the material world but propelled by mythic possibilities. What emerges from this logic of meaning (i.e., the wit in seeming idiocy) is a paradox, the idea of intelligence cloaked with idiocy and possessing potentiality for swinging either way with that tense uncertainty that always conditions embottlement.

Heath's characterization emphasizes the potentiality in embottlement. It is that notion which informs his vision in his most recent work, *The Ministry of Hope. Hope* continues the life story of Kwaku as he leaves New Amsterdam in search of fortune in Georgetown, the Guyanese capital. *Hope* also marks Heath's first direct portrayal of the Guyanese political landscape. The story of how Kwaku, a high school dropout and failed healer, arrives in Georgetown to acquire wealth and cause the fall of the country's Minister of Hope has the mark of comedy. However, in the novel, Kwaku becomes symptomatic of a national crisis as well as the symbol of hope.

Referred by a former client to her son, who is now the Permanent Secretary for the Ministry of Hope, Kwaku leaves his family in New Amsterdam to pursue a trading business in Georgetown. He is associated with Anansi, the trickster (149); Kwaku calls himself "Lord of Confusion" (36), and, by feigning idiocy, "he had become the Prince of dissembling and the Fool who flaunted his flawed literacy, while taking in everything that went on around him" (63). Being an equivocator, Kwaku is willing to meet the challenge of surviving in the city on his own terms. He plans to seek honest work, feed his family, and love his blind wife. Although he arrives in Georgetown desiring to curb his propensity for falsehood and begin a new life, after a few hours in the city, Kwaku realizes that Georgetown is full of corrupt government officials and citizens ready to take advantage of the naïve. He realizes that he must go back to his element in order to survive: "Kwaku had decided to revive his habit of lying extravagantly. After all, what had he encountered since his arrival in Georgetown but extravagant behavior? He had come home! He had found his level at last! . . . There could be no doubt that the town was full of Kwakus, better educated than he, no doubt, but branded with the unmistakable mark of the peculiar breed" (41). But apart from inserting Kwaku into a society where his dissembling lifestyle would thrive, this is Heath's way of commenting on modern Guyanese society where confidence tricksters and duplicitous public servants hold sway.

Though sometimes he wishes he could "curb his tongue, even if he had to chain it" (*Kwaku* 11), Kwaku sees his tendency to create fiction from fact as a necessary act of living. He is aware that he is possessed by Bakoo and only wishes that he could experience the embottled figure in its benevolent aspect: "If only he [Kwaku] could control it [his Bakoo inspiration], suppress its malevolent tendency, so that it came to him in a pure state!" (*Hope* 42). He does cultivate Bakoo's benevolence, scheming his way through ministerial offices, resuming his dubious healing practice, and sharing his resources with his family and acquaintances. In the midst of Kwaku's success is a country tense with boundary disputes with Venezuela, as well as an upcoming election where the Creoles and the East Indians clash over power, and Amerindians are left to their fate in the hinterland.

Kwaku's forced reversal to his old self upon arrival in the city becomes a metaphor for a national ideal betrayed by a corrupt and manipulative political class interested in amassing wealth and power in the newly independent nation, represented by Georgetown. As Ben, the protagonist in *Orealla*, another novel by Heath, muses, "*the town will be our downfall*" (211; original emphasis). Even though the narrator in *Hope* follows Kwaku's scandalous rise to wealth and influence with irony, there is no doubt that it is in Kwaku that Heath posits hope. The Ministry of Hope, from which the novel derives its title, is also the government department in which most of the characters, including the Permanent Secretary, who is Kwaku's supervisor and benefactor, work. The ministry earns its unofficial name because it is administered by a Minister without portfolio. As the narrator explains, "It needs little imagination to discern that the words 'of Hope' in this connection are the equivalent of 'without Hope'. . . . The Minister without portfolio, in short, presided over a Ministry without hope and the Permanent Secretary, his Right Hand Man, was wont to sit on his left hand at important meetings with other heads of Ministries" (45–46). Without a specific policy agenda, the ministry flounders, ruining the lives of its staff. Kwaku survives by quitting his messenger job there. Thus, hope lies in a timely escape from the constricting environment and using the resources in that milieu to chart a different course—the paradoxically fragile and volatile state of Bakoo's embottlement.

Bakoo, Durga, and Old Higue as Guyanese lore figures do not function as mere folkloric materials appearing in Heath's novels. Indeed, they do not overtly announce themselves as such. Rather, Heath works with the figures as agents of meaning. In *A Man Come Home*, Bird Foster enters into a covenant with Water Mama or Fairmaid who rewards him with wealth. His close friend Gee does not know about Bird's new aquatic alliance but believes that his friend's sudden wealth must be from a supernatural source and goes ahead to recount: "I know a man who had a bakoo. . . . All of a sudden this man get a lot of money. He used to buy bananas to feed this bakoo 'pon. And one day the bakoo escape from the bottle he used to keep it in and smash up everything in the man house. From that day he couldn't sleep at night. He start imagining this bakoo come back to kill he. In the end he go mad" (68). The critical aspect of this passage is Gee's casual narration of an acquaintance's possession of Bakoo. The phenomenon is so sewn into the consciousness of the folk that the novel does not attempt to qualify the story. If it is not Fairmaid, it is Bakoo, neither removed from the everyday encounters of the folk.

The idea of embottlement attempts to accentuate Heath's concept of "anxiety lore" as not just a category of African Guyanese mythic repertoire but an aesthetic construct that informs characterization in his writings. It is true that there are many thematic pursuits in his novels, the condition of women possibly the most prominent, but Heath's narratives make a strong case that the African Caribbean apprehension of reality subsists on an intricate network of the several strands of experience that make up the society's cultural consciousness. This consciousness is informed by the history of the Caribbean, the African heritage, and some aspects of the European tradition. Heath's novels circumvent the conventional notion of the form by clearly mapping realism different from the traditional Western "formal realism." Whether called "magical" or "critical" realism, the important thing is that this Guyanese writer has evolved a way of representing the cultural consciousness of his community, a consciousness embedded in its mythic imagination. Yet even more significantly, his writings compel us to enter into that consciousness in order to translate its peculiar grammar of meaning.

− THREE −

Wilson Harris

Dream Worlds and the Oral Imagination

I would suggest that we need to see the future as the parent of time in alternative fictions to robot linearity. When the future parents the past—as the ancient Maya may have perceived it in my understanding of their *stelae* or milestones that are *not* milestones in a progressive or linear sense—then fiction acquires new, creative roots in time and the past presents itself as ceaselessly partial and unfinished. As one senses the body of the wounded past one may also sense simultaneously gestating resources of tradition that we may easily eclipse or forfeit. The tendency in cultures to overlook or bypass such a gestation may indicate a terror in facing the Nemesis of bondage, the way cultures are bonded in tyranny.

—Wilson Harris, in Charles H. Rowell, "An Interview with Wilson Harris" (emphasis in original)

A dynamic notion of realism and cultural identity informs the vision of the Caribbean writer. For Wilson Harris, an authentic representation of cultural consciousness emanates from consciousness cognizant of what he refers to as the "mystery of reality" (*Womb* 71). The artist faces the challenge of representing through language what is perceived in both conscious and subconscious states of existence. The subconscious perception, Harris states, is not secondary or even contrary to the conscious; rather, both exist in a continuum of experience. Not only does Harris make this important clarification concerning the nature of realism in art, but he goes further to situate the concept within a historical framework that sees its origins in political conquests and cultural practices that dehumanize others: "The narrow basis of realism, as an art that mirrors common-sense day or pigmented identity, tends inevitably to polarize cultures or to reinforce eclipses of otherness within legacies of conquest that rule the world. In so doing it also voids a capacity for the true marriage of like to like within a multi-cultural universe" (*Womb* 55). There is a justification for the rejection of such a narrow view of realism, especially as it pertains to non-European literature and its relationship to Western art. For instance, part of the ideological basis for Europeans' enslavement of Africans and the appropriation of Native Indian territories in the Americas was the Europeans' stigmatization of the worldview of the other as irrational and superstitious. Once they peddled this false notion, it was easy to justify or rationalize the colonization of others' territories.

For the Caribbean, the issue of defining realism in the novel is urgent. A pragmatic discourse on cultural consciousness is a practical necessity due to the confluence of cultures—Amerindian, Asian, European, and African—in the region. Harris's writings—critical essays and novels—are efforts to counter a hegemonic discourse that ignores this multicultural perspective; they advance a Caribbean imagination that subsists on a realism where time, place, and action are neither separate entities nor categorized in any order that suggests a clear division between fact and fiction. Rather, the realism consciously dislocates the three "unities" through a process of defamiliarization. I broadly refer to this process as enchantment.

Here I am interested in two aspects of Harris's work: his use of enchantment as an oral narrative technique made manifest through a memory-dream idiom and his deployment of the African mask idiom for character development and representation. These two aspects of his writing are framed by Harris's notion of "literacy of the imagination," which he argues is the precondition for a meaningful representation of the various cultural and historical traditions that converge in the Caribbean.

Enchantment is not necessarily synonymous with magical realism, a term more commonly used in discussions of the type of narratives written by key Latin American writers such as Gabriel García Márquez, Isabel Allende, and Alejo Carpentier. Magical realism emphasizes the way in which events and characters in narrative exceed the "normal" by operating within a typology that, according to David K. Danow, ranges "from the fantastic to the hyperbolic, and from the improbable to the possible" (67). Although the narratives of Harris sometimes seem to exhibit this characteristic, through his intensification of aural and visual images, it would be misleading to conclude that his works belong to the "poetics of excess" said to typify magical realism (ibid.). Neither are his novels mere fantasy novels once the deep philosophical and political truths that Harris embeds in his metaphors and images are understood.

Consequently, enchantment is the way a narrative disrupts the ease with which we understand the world and is not necessarily about a narrative's capability to transport the reader to an extraordinary realm of reality. Mark A. Schneider puts the term "enchantment" in descriptive form when he states, "We become enchanted . . . when we are confronted by circumstances or occurrences so peculiar and so beyond our present understanding as to leave us convinced that, *were* they to be understood, our image of how the world operates would be radically transformed" (3). Here peculiar occurrences or situations in the narrative are a result of transformations of the familiar into new forms that challenge one's perception. The familiar becomes the strange, and one is compelled to see the world only as the novelist would show it, understanding just enough to realize that one may never fully comprehend one's world. Discussing Harris's fiction, Hena Maes-Jelinek describes this aspect as "a keen sensitivity to the material world which leads to the perception of an immaterial world" (*West Indian Literature* 189–90).

In the imaginative typology that defines Wilson Harris's narrative world, "New World" is not just the name given to the Americas with its peculiar history of dispossession, slavery, and colonization; the term also points to the radical transformation of this seemingly familiar territory into an entirely new and "strange" terrain, at once geographically contained yet global in its cultural boundaries. What happens in Guyana resonates with what happens in Nigeria, the United Kingdom, Singapore, or any other part of the globe, and historic figures are seen not merely in the past but as they exist in the present. The surprise, and sometimes uneasiness, the reader experiences on exposure to the mystery of an otherwise known world is the cornerstone of enchantment in Harris's narratives.

These narratives challenge the integrity of the hegemonic type of fiction that is also described as "real." Even though the Aristotelian poetics that prescribes a unity of time, place, and action and a plot with a clearly defined beginning, conflict and resolution no longer holds sway, its core principle of locating "truth" within the material world still wields a powerful influence on art in the Euro-American tradition. However, as William V. Spanos rightly argues in pointing out the implications of Aristotle's spatialization of time in a work of art, we are supposed to "'see' the universe as a miniaturized ordered and intelligible whole. . . . It [the spatialization] generates aesthetic distance from the dislocating contradictions of life in time" (37). Once this dislocation occurs in the construction of life, it becomes tenuous to quest after representing "true" fiction, that is, a fiction that captures life as it is. In other words, the literary tradition to which Spanos refers is largely founded upon a philosophy that attempts to compartmentalize life as a way of making it understandable or controllable. In this condition, a line between the so-called realism of the novel and the supposedly improbable fiction in myth or epic is drawn. What is not understood is considered strange.

On the contrary, Wilson Harris situates the strange alongside the familiar, thereby opening new possibilities of reality that dissolve sheer binary relations. In his essay "The Writer and Society," Harris questions the validity of a straight demarcation of categories of fiction. Reality, he argues, cannot be defined in oppositions, and time cannot be spatialized as it has been formulated in the Western philosophical tradition. Instead, Harris suggests that reality is an embodiment of paradoxes occurring in limitless space. In this condition, it becomes almost impossible to separate the representation of reality in terms of fiction and nonfiction. He calls the Western form of realism the "*status quo* of realism," while what he formulates as realism, he refers to as the "fiction of reality" (49). Harris treats the latter as a "theatre of insubstantial limits." Of course, as I have already noted, the category "Western," as it pertains to genre, is necessarily separate from its common geopolitical reference. Here it is understood as a mode of representation informed by a certain philosophical notion of being and existence that is empiricist. It is also fair to add that the term "Western" derives its meaning from context, as it is not an entirely homogeneous or neutral concept. The point that Harris's own postulations primarily refer to the classical Western tradition makes clear that the distinction between his construct of realism and the *other* is considerably more aesthetic than geopolitical. In essence, what occurs in his fiction is "a genuine sense of textual syncreticity and transformation" (Griffiths 69).

At first glance, the distinction between "*status quo* of realism" and "fiction of reality" may appear more wordplay than substantive criticism. However, Harris has produced such a volume of creative and scholarly works in which he has consistently engaged in this discourse that it is possible to examine it critically. Harris's imaginative works aim at dislodging hegemonies of thinking by embracing a multicultural consciousness that explores the "mystery of reality." As a Guyanese writer with an acute awareness of the role of Western humanist thinking in the campaign for and perpetration of slavery, colonialism, and their consequences in the Caribbean, Harris unravels the implications of this dark history by centering the ex-colonial subject as both a forced product of a tradition and an iconoclast of that same tradition. I will attempt to examine this tradition in my reading of principally three of his later novels, namely, *Carnival* (1985), *Resurrection at Sorrow Hill* (1993), and *Jonestown* (1996). However, I will also refer to *Palace of the Peacock* (1960), his first published novel, which undoubtedly sets the stage for the aesthetic principle that continues to inform Harris's writings.

To understand Harris's mode of representation in fiction, it will be useful to first mention three motifs or archetypes he has used to articulate what he calls the "drama of consciousness" in which the writer is an active participant. Central to each archetype is the figure of the artist/writer as a voyager who "sets out again and again across a certain territory of primordial but broken recollection in search of a community or species of fiction whose existence he begins to discern" ("Writer and Society" 48). There is a persistent concern with spaces or territories of imagination that the artist must traverse to represent reality effectively. This concern relates to a function that I described earlier as "transgressive," to navigate fossilized and monolithic boundaries of thinking and perception and interrogate dominant paradigms. The three archetypes Harris expounds on have the attributes of embodying multiple tropes of consciousness.

The first figure is Tiresias, the seer in classical Greek mythology, punished by the gods by turning him into a woman for seven years then back to a man. In the land of the dead, he is also the only "living" person who could finally provide a direction of escape for the wearied traveler Ulysses (Odysseus) when he visits the underworld for directions back to Ithaka. Harris gives theoretical significance to this myth by showing how Tiresias symbolizes the imaginative consciousness of the writer:

> What one finds in this drama of consciousness is that Tiresias is the embodiment of death as well as life, masculine as well as feminine, because it is through him that the writer lays bare a fiction corresponding to a community whose wholeness in reality cannot exist except by confessing its own insubstantial limits, thereby invoking not only the horror of disorientation but an implosive compass of freedom as well within such insubstantial limits overlooked by prejudice from the microcosm of society and rejected equally by prejudice from the macrocosm of inanimate nature. (49)

Thus, a rounded reality is one that acknowledges and appropriates the boundlessness of space; the artist's ability to exercise the freedom of seeking out both animate and inanimate "existences" that make up the community's corporeal and intangible world represents this reality.

The second archetype, invoked for its "phenomenon of sensibility" (52), is the encounter of Ulysses and his crew with the fatally enchanting Sirens (*Odyssey* XII.44–254). At the loss of some of his crewmembers, Odysseus escapes from Circe but must literally face the music of the Sirens. While his surviving men save themselves by stopping their ears with wax, the hero is to listen to the enthralling music while tied fast to the ship's mast. As he stands immobilized and driven to distraction by the allure of the Sirens' music, Odysseus's men are responsive neither to his cries to be untied nor to the music. Nevertheless, Odysseus must listen, desiring, as he does so, to heed the enchanting call of the nymphs. This is the crucial moment that Harris uses to demonstrate the phenomenon of sensibility. Here, a community of animate and inanimate attributes forms as Odysseus becomes one with the mast on which he is tied, while he is still the only ear exercising a full consciousness of the music's pleasure and fatal significance. His men, on the other hand, though still rowing and seeing, "can only dream to move with such close proximity to the dreadful command of death or love by acquiring the ear of the deaf. The ear of wood or stone" (54). Odysseus and his men, at this moment, function in a dislocated consciousness where shape and sound, animate and nonanimate entities assume new identities and perform differently from their ordinary functions.

There is more symbolism to the figure of Odysseus than the metaphysical implication of his being tied to the mast. Odysseus is the archetypal wanderer, or explorer, when the reader notes that it is his lust for adventure and wealth that takes him and his men off course to Ithaka in the first place. Homer calls him "the wiliest fighter of the islands" (XXII.1), the "canniest of men" (VIII.160), and "that man skilled in all ways of contending" (I.2). Odysseus is the trickster who becomes "Nohbody" in order to escape Polyphemos, the Cyklops (IX.394–449). Harris interprets him as a Caribbean figure: the impenetrable Amazon and the Orinoco rivers flowing through Guyana are the treacherous landscape with which the writer's imagination must reconcile. Even Odysseus's momentary change of name becomes a metaphor for potentiality that Harris explores through the characters Nameless in *Resurrection* and Idiot Nameless in *Companions of the Day and Night.*

The third illustration of the imaginative consciousness Harris expounds is the Haitian ritual practice of voodoo. Harris focuses on the dance motions when the dancer loses consciousness and enters into a subconscious state, "the womb of space" wherein "all conventional memory is erased and yet in this trance of overlapping spheres of reflection a primordial or deeper function of memory begins to exercise itself within the bloodstream of space" (51). Call it possession or trance, Harris sees the dancer as a "dramatic agent of consciousness," a medium who in that "void of sensation" collapses the division between life within and life without. In relating the significance of voodoo to the archeology of consciousness, Harris writes: "Haitian *vodun* is one of the surviving primitive dances of ancient sacrifice, which, in courting a subconscious community, *sees* its own performance in literal terms—that is, with and through the eyes of 'space': with and through the sculpture of sleeping things which the dancer himself actually expresses and becomes" (51; emphasis in original).[1]

What emerges from the three models explored above is a deliberate displacement of conventional perceptions and interpretations of consciousness. The insubstantial limits of space are crucial to this notion. Human consciousness extends to and becomes the subconscious and vice versa. Such mutual interchange enables the artist to represent existence in all dimensions or manifestations. The linearity of time in the mundane world coalesces with uncharted time in space. In this sphere, there is no absolute present, past, or future. Events and characters exist in moments and each moment, ordinary as it may seem, subsists through the process of dislocated consciousness, in the mood of enchantment.

Harris's three archetypes relate to the aesthetics of oral narrativity. The most obvious is his referencing of mythic figures—Tiresias and Ulysses. Myth provides a viable framework for the artist interested in traversing the conventional boundaries between what is perceived to be real and what is not. Indeed, Ikenna Dieke, in *The Primordial Image*, identifies Harris's narratives as examples of a mythopoetic text that he defines as "a parable of the infinite and the eternal imagination, deriving its basic meaning from the correlative scheme of myth, dream and symbol, and having for its use mythical, allegorical and dream-like modes of thought, which are understood as projections of psychological realities into concrete expressions" (364–65). As G. S. Kirk puts it, although a weakness in the form, "the major avenue to richness and fascination in mythic composition is just the developmental weakness that allows anything to happen" (109). One can only add that, with Harris, the mythic sign is not a capricious invention but one informed by a vision of the universe in which entities that comprise the cosmos materialize in the narrative through the mediation of the artist's imagination. In fact, it is not really a question of the artist's perception of the universe in the ontological sense as much as it is a performance aesthetic that shapes the fluid swing to and from the "real" and the "imagined." In *Myth in Africa*, Okpewho appropriately calls this aesthetic the "mythopoeic fancy" (114). This fancy stems from the notion of play—the ability of the narrator to wield his or her creative genius across imagination's arc that spans from historical through not-so-historical experiences. In Okpewho's words, this fancy

concerns itself with the entire spectrum of the social universe: from issues which translate into *experience* in terms of more or less remote history to those which constitute *existence* in a more transcendent sense. On the one hand the imagination focuses on *actualities* past or present and endeavors progressively to derive from them certain essences which liberate them from the bond of time; on the other hand it grapples with *mysteries* by seeking to explain them in terms of observable reality without however destroying their supra-empirical quality. (114; emphasis in original)

What determines the side of the spectrum the narrative inhabits includes such factors as the nature of the audience—gender, age, ethnicity, and so on—the occasion, and the narrator's personal creative agenda. More importantly, there is a mutual understanding between a performer and the community that, in each performance, these swings can be arbitrary and yet expected.

The imaginative world that Harris presents, like that of many Caribbean writers, pays homage to a gamut of cultural traditions. The oral or folkloric aspects of these traditions, be they the aesthetics of oral performance and mask idioms from Africa or the classical Greek mythologies, receive special attention in Harris's works. The seeming tensions between the oral and written traditions converge in Harris's insistence on a "literacy of the imagination." Harris constructs literacy as consciousness, the knowledge and awareness of existence, histories, and philosophies in asymmetrical relationships that preclude the privileging or preference of one over others. Referring to ancient Maya and African belief systems that embrace multidimensional beings and realities, Harris argues that the consequence of imaginative illiteracy is a world where some societies insist on the superiority of their way of thinking, history, and culture. Other traditions are lost on them, making them ignorant, or illiterate, so to speak ("Literacy and the Imagination" 77). Since the West Indies is home to many traditions—lost, suppressed, dominant—Harris argues elsewhere that the Caribbean writer must rise to constructing identity and defining aesthetics based on the notion "close to the inner universality of the Caribbean man" ("History, Fable and Myth" 157). Obviously, the idea of the West Indian as the prototype of humanity overstates the point, but it accentuates Harris's argument for a different interpretation and usage of traditions and philosophies, especially as it pertains to his homeland.

It is true that Harris's theory of imaginative consciousness seems to rely heavily on writing; nevertheless, its underlying aesthetic principle comes from an open, mythopoetic aesthetic akin to the dominant oral forms among African societies. This principle can best be understood by the idea of a total theater. By total theater, I mean the presentation of an artistic statement through a performance that concurrently utilizes or appeals to auditory, visual, and verbal senses. It is total because, in this enactment, there are no firm lines drawn between forms.[2] The Harrisian principle that allows for the interpenetration of the animate and the inanimate, the "mystery of reality" and the everyday in a vortex of space, is comparable to the theatrical quality of the African oral performance. In this performance, the performer manipulates the text to meet the ever-changing demands of his or her audience. To allow for a satisfactory performance, the artist must go into multidimensional levels of communication. Communication is not a mere telling of a tale; the body and facial gestures, the vocal inflections, the ready presence of song and dance, and the recourse to the spectacular are features in a performance enacted to uplift the cultural consciousness of the community.

Even though Harris imbues his narratives with a global perspective, the constant focus is Guyana, and this suggests his awareness of the bond that exists between artist and community. The community he represents is also a diverse one. Harris pays homage to the African, Amerindian, and Maya roots of his culture through an eclectic application of their individually unique worldviews in his narrative. If sometimes a reader experiences confusion due to the coalescing of these experiences in the narratives, it may well be Harris's way of problematizing the history of Guyana and indeed the Caribbean.

While Harris presents Guyana as a theater of global political manipulations and contests, he also privileges this cultural space as site of his creative muse and aesthetic agenda. Before moving to England in 1959, he worked as a land surveyor, a job that took him on expeditions to the rainforest interior of Guyana. The firsthand encounters with the vegetation became a catalyst for his wider interest in the mystical connection between the environment and Guyanese identity. In an interview with fellow Guyanese writer Fred D'Aguiar, for example, Harris recalls one such surveying assignment, this time on the Cuyuni River, and its significance:

> This expedition was a revelation to me: multitudinous forests I had never seen before, the whisper or sigh of a tree with a tone or rhythm I had never known, real (it seemed) and unreal footsteps in the shoe of a cracking branch, mysterious play in the rivers at nights, distant rain bringing the sound of approaching fire in the whispering leaves, horses' hooves on water on rock, the bark of dogs of technology in the bruised tumult of a

waterfall. . . . Much more that witnessed to the living water and land one
had assumed to be *insentient* in the coastal and urban regions. This was
another planet, a *living*, unpredictable planet. (76; emphasis in original)

To Harris, the Guyanese landscape not only sustains a diverse ecosys-
tem; the immense diversity seems to correlate with his aesthetic ideology that promotes the interrelatedness of various life forms, myths, and
legends.

Even before his encounters in the bush as a surveyor, Harris had undergone other personal experiences that very much defined the prominence
of Guyanese landscapes, especially the interior, in his writings. Harris lost
his father when he was two years old. Four years later, his stepfather vanished in the Guyana forest. Reflecting on the significance of this tragic
turn of events to his writing career, Harris states: "My stepfather's disappearance in that immense interior when I was a child was the beginning
of an involvement with the enigma of quests and journeys through visible into invisible worlds that become themselves slowly visible to require
further penetration into other invisible worlds without end or finality"
("Wilson Harris" 122). Granted, a writer's explanation of the sources of
meaning in his writings is not necessarily the final word on such writings;
yet it would seem that Harris's childhood losses, the stepfather's disappearance, are etched deeply in his consciousness, inspiring a large body of
works that highlight landscapes fraught with anxiety and uncertainty. In
his essay "Tradition and the West Indian Novel," Harris relates this sense
of inconclusiveness to the subject of Caribbean identity. The Caribbean as
the confluence of various civilizations, with a long history of violent conquests, appropriations, and indigenous adaptations, resists a simple lineal
or homogeneous narrative. "The question is," Harris poses, "how can one
begin to reconcile the broken parts of such an enormous heritage, especially when those broken parts appear very often like a grotesque series
of adventures, volcanic in its precipitate efforts as well as human in its
vulnerable settlements?" (142). Ultimately, he argues that it is important
that a West Indian consciousness be informed by this series of cultural and
historical ruptures.

Masks and Dreamscapes of the Imagination

Palace of the Peacock, the first in the Guyana Quartet, effectively begins
Harris's lifelong artistic campaign to represent the Caribbean world in

that pluralistic mode and articulate Caribbean poetics informed by the various strands of history, culture, and beliefs present in the region. An unnamed first-person narrator who disappears for most of the story, his older brother Donne, and a boat crew of eight men relive an expedition into the Guyanese interior, ostensibly in search of treasures hidden among the Amerindian "folks." In the space of the seven days of the journey, the characters' lives—their death and resurrection—and their perilous excursion become an allegorical journey toward the construction of a New World consciousness or, as the narrator puts it, "the creation of the windows of the universe" (111).

Harris brings together the different actors on the Caribbean stage to reprise their roles and find opportunity for transformation and redemption. Donne, the leader of the group, is the conquistador in search of wealth and power who has little regard for the poor folks he oppresses. He proudly tells the dreaming narrator, "One has to be a devil to survive. I'm the last landlord. I tell you I fight everything in nature, flood, drought, chicken hawk, rat, beast and woman. I'm everything. Midwife, yes, doctor, yes, gaoler, judge, hangman, every blasted thing to the labouring people" (22). Because of Donne's obsession with power ("Rule the land . . . And you rule the world" [23]) and self-centeredness, he does not grasp how deeply his fate is tied to his lowly crew's.

Four of the eight crew members—Schomburgh, Cameron, Vigilance, and Carroll—are blood relatives, and many in the crew come from Sorrow Hill, a poor community at the foot of a waterfall in the forest. While Donne is abusive and thus alienated from people around him, the narrator takes time to describe the web of relationships among the crew, not only as a contrast to their leader but also as a pointer to the intricate mix of histories that cut across ethnicities and class. The relationship between Cameron, who appears to possess some of Donne's lust for power and freedom, and Schomburgh, the oldest and the boat's bowman, is one example of this admixing, which the narrator presents for deeper nationalist significance. According to the narrator:

> Cameron's great-grandfather had been a dour Scot, and his great-grandmother an African slave and mistress. Cameron was related to Schomburgh . . . and it was well-known that Schomburgh's great-grandfather had come from Germany, and his great-grandmother was an Arawak American Indian. The whole crew was one spiritual family living and dying together in a common grave out of which they had sprung again from the same soul and womb as it were. (39)

At first, one may interrogate the imbalance of power between the African slave and mistress of Cameron's Scottish ancestor. However, the narrator's matter-of-fact description of that relationship, the deliberate emphasis on their ethnicities, and the editorial on what their associations mean as Guyanese are the precursors to Harris's march toward a new notion of the West Indies, a new identity that embraces cross-racial and cultural ruptures and looks beyond economic or historical inequities.

Not that Harris ignores the reality of historical injustices meted to certain ethnicities or to present-day minority people-groups. On the contrary, Harris is keenly interested in retrieving the grotesque quirks of history, the tragic outcomes of eras, movements, and historical or mythic figures who fail to grapple with what he conceptualizes as an ever-evolving, nonstatic, and multidimensional universe. Thus, in the West Indian experience, the artist must insist on representing the emerging inequities and conflicts of the post-Columbian world, as well as the limitless possibilities evinced by the convergence of world cultures and peoples in one "womb" of humanity. In the novel, the mythical "Palace of the Peacock" is the womb. There, as Donne makes the ascent to a room, he encounters the young "craftman of God" with a hammer, chisel, and saw. Donne is literally recreated: he feels himself "sliced with this skeleton-saw by the craftman of God in the windowpane of his eye" and realizes that "the chisel and the saw in the room had touched him and done something in the wind and the sun to make him anew" (102). He abandons his self-centeredness and realizes that he is part of a larger cosmic family.

One important aspect of *Palace* is that it is a dream-sequenced narrative. The unnamed narrator calls Donne his older brother, but because the narrator fuses nonlineal time with animate and inanimate beings, Donne sometimes appears as the narrator's twin, sometimes in present time, otherwise in the future or past. Even then, it is not clear if Donne is not a projection of an idea through the sublimated narrator. Nevertheless, the ability of the characters to enter into spaces and times seamlessly marks the beginning of Harris's exploration of a counternarrative aesthetic. In my reading of *Carnival*, I would like to consider the novelist's use of the African mask idiom and the institution of carnival as a cultural manifestation of this idiom.

As Aldrick Prospect, a major Afro Caribbean character in Earl Lovelace's novel *The Dragon Can't Dance*, puts on his carnival dragon costume, he does not see the event as an ordinary annual entertainment but rather internalizes the festival as a reenactment of African mask theater; every year he feels "a sense of entering a sacred mask that invested him with an ancestral authority to uphold before the people of [the] hill" (120). Aldrick's experience of this ancestral consciousness emanates from his awareness of the symbolism of the African masquerade. Carnival operates as "a symbol of social and historical transformation" (Paravisini-Gebert 235). The appropriation of power and the desire to serve as guide to his impoverished people, the Hill community, is in recognition of the mask in African ritual-drama as a cosmic agent that bridges the gap between the finite consciousness of the living and the limitless and mysterious space occupied by the unborn and the dead.

However, the mask has an added value: "A masked figure at a festival," Oyin Ogunba writes in his essay on African festival theater, "has by his mere appearance created a situation of potential dramatic value. . . . Since he is a visitor from the land of the spirits, it is the atmosphere which his sheer presence creates that generates the drama" (23). The African mask theater also provides an opportunity for the community to assume momentarily the personality of the ancestors and other personages that inhabit the chthonian realm. The members of the community who at the festival surrender themselves to be transported into the world of the spirits are also conscious (even if only before their unconscious transition into infinite space) of the dramatic value of the ceremony, for is it not also an occasion for the celebration of the artistic resources of the land? This may conflict with a prevailing tendency to see the mask theater purely through the mirror of ritual aesthetics.[3] However, it needs to be said that the mask operates as a manifestation of the *play* essence of the theater. Although crucial to reconciling the various constituents of the community's sense of being, masquerades also afford performers the dramatic opportunity to assume new roles and new voices, as well as to solicit a peculiar artistic response from the audience. Even when the community reenacts an historic incident, it does not entirely lose sight of the sheer spectacle that this evocation conjures.

How, then, does Harris's *Carnival* draw from the African mask idiom? The answer lies with Everyman Masters, the novel's ubiquitous character whose consciousness inhabits and directs the narration by Jonathan Weyl. Masters, the product of a forbidden sexual liaison between a colored woman and a white man in the plantation community of New Forest, is mistakenly killed by the husband of a woman who assumes him to be her abusive overseer. However, he reemerges in London and twenty-five years later is stabbed to death a second time by an unknown assailant after a sexual encounter with his female co-tenant on his sixty-fifth birthday.[4] On news of Masters's death, the narrator, a younger friend of Masters, notes that he was "possessed by lucid dreams that intermingled fact with imaginative truth" (11) about the deceased. Therefore, he begins writing Masters's biography or, as Masters calls Weyl's task, a "biography of spirit." To write this biography, Masters leads young Weyl through time to relive Masters's life and see Weyl's own future where he meets Amaryllis, his future wife. With an overriding sense of Dante's *Divine Comedy*, Masters puts on the mask of a guide and leads Jonathan through the inferno and purgatory of his life, a journey that acquires deeper significance when Masters tells his charge at the conclusion of the first chapter, "Think of men and women from all walks of life who become victims, innocent victims. . . . How to identify those who are guilty, acquit those who are innocent! How to perceive the morality of Carnival within a universal plague of violence! That is our play. We shall descend, ascend, we shall travel around the globe. . . . These are the facts on which the judgement of spirit rests" (10). The abnormal circumstances of Masters's birth and educational upbringing in the colonial New Forest society, and the equally abnormal circumstance of Weyl's birth and the death of his father, Martin Weyl, are tales of an oppressive society that masks its failures through several layers of contradicting morality and violent impositions. Masters takes his charge to unveil the masks, and the "judgement of spirits" comes about through this unveiling.

However, the morality of carnival is such that it allows for an unveiling (paradoxically through the concealing nature of the mask) without guaranteeing permanence for what it reveals. In a worldview that abhors fossilizing thought and deed, the mask is a powerful idiom that reveals only for the moment it is evoked. Nothing is completely resolved, no image whole. As Masters tells his ward, "the partial image . . . frees us from the absolutes that clothe our memory and to reveal a potential that has always been there for mutual rebirth within conflicting, dying, hollow generations" (44–45).[5] Consequently, the novel's individual narratives attempt to associate with each other but ultimately do not, thereby precluding a sense of closure.

Like the seer Tiresias, Everyman Masters and Jonathan Weyl have the capacity to see beyond their time. Weyl is active in the present but privy to the past; Masters, through the mediumistic agency of dream, is an arch visionary who is a privileged participant in the past as well as guide to Weyl in Weyl's relocated consciousness into that past. Masters is also able to see trends of the future, some of which offer redemption for the mistakes of the past. Harris imbues Masters with wisdom similar to that of the mythic figure. He perceives the contradictions of his twentieth-century society and is able to articulate the deeper significance of incidents that occur in the society through his "capacity to revisit occasions, to return again and again to vacancies of memory and to first things and last things that are neither last nor first in the kingdom of spirit" (124). Like his mythic predecessor, Masters is the lone dead figure who can give direction or insight to his living inquirer from the "kingdom of spirit."

Part of the insight Masters offers is how Jonathan understands New Forest history and how racial polarization in the society due to slavery has undermined the progress of the community and the individual. Interestingly, this lesson comes through revisiting the life of the elder Weyl, Martin, a young colored lawyer who befriends Jennifer, a "perhaps white" woman (90). At twenty-five, Weyl is forced to marry Jennifer when an "outraged middle-class establishment" (75) discovers that she is three months pregnant. To avoid ostracism and loss of clientele, Weyl marries Jennifer; but the marriage only leaves the couple with the depressing feeling of being pawns in their community's philistine morality. Masters calls the unwanted child, Jonathan, a "child of carnival." Jonathan, now viewing the circumstances of his birth through the privileged eyes of Masters, writes of the real cause of the problem: "It had all started when a plantation society stood at their backs and peered over their shoulders into their private lives, at their shadowy bodies of intercourse. Shadows! Who actually lay with whom? Who had made love to whom? It was almost as if his [Martin's] *love* for the woman he was forced to marry was immaterial. *They must marry;* they must marry or else" (75–76; original emphasis).

The lingering echoes of slavery appear here as a middle-class establishment seeking revenge on a colored man who dares overstep the color line in the New Forest society by enforcing a dubious morality code set up by the former white slave owner. The code, Masters tells Jonathan, is the society's mask for hiding its shame and embarrassment of the past. It is a subterfuge for avoiding change or taking responsibility. Ultimately, it protects the interests of the status quo. However, the code is a "diseased" mask, as Masters tells the narrator, which is used to "suppress the challenge of disturbing inner truth that transcends circumstantial appearance" (84). Martin Weyl also wears a mask, the mask of "Doubting Thomas," fashioned after the figure of the biblical apostle Thomas, who in the novel becomes an archetype for the various misfortunes—economic, educational, social, and religious—that befall the New Forest ex-colonial. He must preserve the hollow morality of his peers, even if such sentiment "seemed of little importance in a world in depression [the child was born in 1932], a world of common law wives in the Market-place labouring folk" (75), and even if he was uncertain and questioned the wisdom of it all.

Masters portrays Martin Weyl as a tragic Thomas figure. He is a brilliant man torn between accepting the strictures of the establishment and breaking away from them in order to expose their hypocrisy. He understands the diverse cultural experience of his South American society and questions the enthronement of one aspect of the society's culture and belief system over the entire community. When Weyl chooses to defend an Amerindian prince accused of matricide, his controversial decision leads to his death. The case is a classic example of a clash of cultures and the consequence of wielding one belief system as an oppressive tool for controlling weaker ones. The Amerindian's mother is dying of cancer and the native medium, Kanaima, commands the man to release his mother from the pain and send her onward to the other life. In carrying out the spirit's command, he breaches the colonial English law that governs New Forest, a law the Amerindian does not understand and which the colonial court sees as an opportunity to civilize a "savage heart." The Amerindian's case worsens by his inability to speak the language and the blunders by the court interpreters whose competence in the English language is so mediocre that their translation of the defendant's words proves ineffective.

Weyl fights to save the Amerindian's life by trying to get the court to understand the belief that drives a son to kill his mother. He argues that though the colonial law is in effect among the conquered natives, it should not invalidate the sacred laws by which the people themselves live. The judge finds the accused man guilty despite Weyl's effort, and, minutes later, the narrator presents the death of his father as a sacrifice to a pervasive and oppressive colonial system:

[H]e was a figure of Carnival dance, a secretive chained boulder drenched in Waterfall Oracle. He had forgotten to disrobe and still wore his gown and wig like sackcloth and bleached autumn snow. He blundered into the road and was knocked to the ground by a cyclist before receiving a frightful blow on the head (crushed dream-eggshell) from the iron wheel of a dray cart. It ran over him even as the alarmed shadow of the half-prancing donkey or mule or horse that drew the cart engulfed him. Was it shadow-animal or shadow-cart? (The personality or shadow of the animal that pulled the shadow-vehicle was never established, as if to embroider into sphinx-like proportion the profligacy of the boulder-dance written into my father's death. Pinned to a wall, pinned to a road, yet limbs flung apart, dancing, collapsing in space.) (107–8)[6]

The symbolism of the attorney dying in the robe of the legal system that crushes him is not lost on the reader. The rigidity of that system's law, the same absolutism that informs nations that overrun and acquire sovereign peoples as their colonies, is the predator that devours Weyl. His lawyer's robe hangs upon him as sackcloth, a somber symbol of his stature as a tragic figure who mourns for the misunderstood and subjugated colored peoples of New Forest.

Characterization in *Carnival* is based on the dramatic value of the mask in African theater. The masquerade event provides the community of the living an opportunity to share in the world of the dead and the unborn by assuming their personage. The two narrative agents, Everyman Masters and Jonathan Weyl, constantly acquire the voice and consciousness of other characters in the novel and sometimes go further to create archetypes that represent concepts.[7] First, there is the symbolism in Everyman's name. His consciousness is nobody's in particular. Although Weyl's biography project is on Masters, Masters nonetheless attaches and distances himself at will from the events he witnesses.

In the novel, he lives four lives, each with a distinct impact on the narrative. Masters the first is the New Forest Carnival Child, the product of an apparent rape of a black plantation woman by her white boss. Masters chooses to turn the humiliation of his birth into power by immersing himself in the colonial system through the "disease" he calls "Ambition," the driving force for all territorial annexations and ideological hegemonies throughout the globe. He goes through an arduous colonial education where he sees through the hypocrisy of the system, and he emerges neither totally assimilated nor estranged from it. He becomes an overseer of a plantation and, like his white counterparts, abuses his position by sleeping with the female workers. Though stabbed to death due to mistaken identity, it is clear that he does not deny his complicity in such abusive relations. Masters the second appears in London where by a quirk of fate he cavorts with a white woman who seems to be wearing the mask of the black plantation woman who had stabbed him. He is mysteriously killed again. Then he emerges the third time as Jonathan's guide through time and, finally, as a Lazarus archetype rising from the inferno of the world's tragedies to lead Jonathan and his bride, Amaryllis, through the purgatory of hope. In each of these incarnations, he does not lose sight of his other lives, and consequently he exists as a multiple personality.

Another aspect of the carnival masking in the novel is the almost inseparable bond between Masters and the younger Weyl. Nowhere is this bond more keenly felt than in the narrative process. In the novel, both characters use the narrative "I" interchangeably, though Masters's statements generally appear in quotation marks. However, it is not so much the interchange of voice as the fact that, as the novel progresses, the thoughts of the "designated" narrator and biographer, Jonathan, merge into the statements of Masters. Although Jonathan is the writer, it is Masters who provides him with guidance: "he [Masters] stood at my elbow as I wrote of him, and guided me into the seemingly impossible realms" (83). Furthermore, Jonathan abdicates any kind of authority in the writing of the story. In fact, he tells the reader that, in the carnival frame of his writing, he is a creation of the character-masks that he writes about:

> Indeed in a real and unreal sense he [Masters] and other character-masks were the joint authors of Carnival and I was their creation. They drew me to surrender myself to them.
>
> My hand was suffused as I wrote by their parallel hands, my eyes as I looked around by their parallel eyes. (27)

Yet the narrator maintains a concrete individuality; after all, his birth and parts of his life story feature prominently in the narrative. Harris is exploring the dialectic between the writer's imagination and art. Just as the participant in carnival is temporarily "captured" by the spirit of the character, the artist's work can also become the artist and vice versa. Such a situation is especially likely in an aesthetic that abhors inflexible boundaries and celebrates a multidimensional artistic imagination.

Shifting Spaces and Transcultural Iconographies

The novels *Resurrection at Sorrow Hill* and *Jonestown* are examples of Harris problematizing the reality of the writer existing as a real person and equally written into his or her fictive world. For one, the step transforms the nature of the genre. Removing the distance between the writer of a story who lives in the real world and the narrative voice(s) that tell a story as fiction transforms the novel as a literary form. The effectiveness of a work as fiction mainly depends on its reception as an imitation of everyday language in action performed by imaginary characters. Even where authorial or editorial comments exist, the fictive context limits the extent to which the author (as in the person whose name appears on the cover of the book) is associated with the comments. But that separation of the actual author from the imagined one collapses in *Resurrection*. A dated prefatory note signed by "WH" notes: "I have edited Hope's asylum book *Resurrection at Sorrow Hill* at his request." Hope is a character in *Resurrection* who is engaged in documenting incidents in a mental asylum where he, too, is an inmate. After some remarks on the characters in Hope's book, WH tells the reader that he was "aware" as he "read Hope's book" of the premise on which Hope delineated his characters. This is the crossroads of "fiction" and "factuality": there is the book *Resurrection at Sorrow Hill* that one finds in a bookstore or library written by Wilson Harris (WH?); there is a story of similar title edited by WH that is ostensibly written by Hope, a character in Harris's novel. Unlike Harris, whom we can locate historically, there is no record of Hope nor of the characters in Hope's *Resurrection at Sorrow Hill,* though the author claims factuality for his account of events and persons at the asylum. We are certain that they are fictive just as we are certain that Wilson Harris is a Guyanese writer residing in Britain with his wife, Margaret. But how certain are we?

Harris and Hope's existence falls within the "fiction of reality" paradigm. Harris's realist paradigm views life or global history as a series of occurrences that in themselves have the makings of a fiction but are at the same time very much part of the material consciousness. His is a deliberately "dislocated" consciousness. If Harris the novelist, at the outset of his composition, writes himself into his fictive work by representing himself as his characters' collaborator, it effectively discourages his readers from approaching the work with a received familiarity. This is neither a fictive biography nor an autobiography, yet the prefatory note makes the work both.[8] Even in Hope's asylum book, he struggles with one of the inmates, Nameless, who insists on writing himself into the book (171). Such an arrangement accentuates Harris's aesthetic proposition in which the artist transcends categorical boundaries and embraces the entire spectrum of perception that constitutes imagination.

Space is critical in Harris's exploration of the unfettered imagination. Its mystery and vastness are the gateways through which Harris's creative energy finds release. Space cannot be grasped totally; rather, it possesses the potential for unifying the various constituents of animate and inanimate "life" through its creative power. As Hope wonders in his Dream-book, "Is space itself a giant shell, a giant surrogate ear of multidimensional God? Is space the inverse ventriloquist organ that the birds of the air tap when they sing, when they mimic spiritual ecstasy, spiritual torment, spiritual lament?" (45). In *Resurrection,* a careful delineation of this space manifests itself in the "Constellation of Tiresias." Daemon, the doctor in charge of the asylum in Sorrow Hill, a community that, like New

Forest, "was born of a precipitation from voyages and movements of peoples descending from ancient America, from Renaissance Europe, from the Siberian Straits, from Africa, from India, from Asia" (4), is devastated by his wife Ruth's death by drowning. In grief, he sets up an astrological observatory where every night he peers into the skies, apparently in search of his lost wife. Hope suggests to Daemon's "blind, seeing" grandmother to turn her grandson's instrument "into an eye of generations . . . [that] peer into every crevice of fear, the fear of absolute extinction that haunts humanity as it seeks a home in space, the home of the surviving Soul" (6). It is an eye on human history that extends its scope beyond the material plane to survey other spheres of existence. Daemon's grandmother, by acquiring "telescopic antennae of vision" (6), possesses the mystical attributes of the mythic Tiresias and is transformed into being the center of the overarching spheres. The constellation (of Tiresias), she remarks in her narrative voice, would "draw together a confluence of spaces, inner spaces, outer spaces, obsessions, loves, jealousies, neuroses, paranoia, that plague humanity" (6). It is within and through the constellation that the asylum characters recreate their real and assumed personalities. Hope is seen as a "myth-maker" while Sorrow Hill is "a place of myth in that every invention of truth deepened one's apprehension of the gravity of truth" (3). Not only does the constellation signify the interstitial realm between fiction and factuality in which the novel's action is set, but it also reinforces Harris's idea of literate imagination liberated from contrived boundaries.

The world in *Resurrection* is full of possibilities. Each inmate's life in the asylum presents a conclusive yet unfolding drama. Hope's Dream-book pries into the subconscious of all the inmates to reveal their individual fears as well as demonstrate how all of them, despite the uniqueness of the circumstances that bring them to the asylum, are objects in the huge canvas of world history. Christopher D'eath, an engineer sent to replace an ailing Hope at the power station in Sorrow Hill, arrives with his beautiful wife, Butterfly. Harris converts their arrival into an occasion for an allegorical message, myth-making, and religious iconoclasm. Like the old Donne in *Palace of the Peacock,* lust for power and fame fuels D'eath's arrival at the station. His ambition is to be "Mr. Universe" and his wife, "Miss World." Sorrow Hill is a lush El Dorado to be exploited, his angelic wife a trophy to be kept and protected. Yet Hope and Butterfly are attracted to each other and begin a secret relationship that, despite its illegitimacy, is consummated in metaphysical terms.

Harris presents Christopher D'eath as an adversary to the unpretentious and passionate love that Hope and Butterfly risk their lives to celebrate. In fact, the danger lies more in the paradoxical attributes in the engineer's names. As Christopher, he is a "witness to the resurrection," that is, Christ's resurrection. As D'eath, he is a "witness to suicidal lust and the perversity of survival" (23). The significance of this naming intensifies when, in a dreamlike state, D'eath shoots to kill Hope and Butterfly on discovering them in a sexual lair. D'eath, whose name might as well be Death, experiences few "Christopher-moods of tenderness" (23). His driving force, suicidal in intensity, turns him into a noncaring individual possessed by the spirit of acquisition. He comes to Sorrow Hill to "make a quick *killing*" (22; emphasis added). Hope describes him as a jailer, and, among the spaces that make up Hope's Constellation, D'eath exists in the "Spider planet" because of his ruthless desire to snare wealth and hold absolute control over Butterfly.

In contrast, Hope and Butterfly exist in the parallel Resurrection planet. Their lives possess the redemptive value of the resurrection in Sorrow Hill. Resurrection, as Daemon's seer grandmother visualizes it, is "a numinous embodiment of potential creativity in the community" (9). If D'eath represents the ruthless acquisition and display of power and wealth that are the very catalysts of the colonization and impoverishment of Guyana and other South American nations by European conquistadors, then his wife and her lover offer possibility of freedom. For Hope liberates Butterfly from the stranglehold of D'eath, who sees her as a trophy and investment and reduces their sexual relation to a cheerless one: "D'eath's mechanics of sex (a metallic key in a metallic object or door) ran in discordant but powerful unison with his [Hope's] tremor or penetrative insight into the mystery or the grain of living nature" (26). Harris does not concern himself with the morality of the liaison between Butterfly and Hope. Instead, the affair attains significance on two levels of meaning. First, it is the adversarial relationship between Hope and D'eath or, in Christian philosophical thought, between Christ and death that is heightened. At the end, D'eath must be incarcerated for seven years to purge him of his lusts and make him part of Resurrection planet. The seven years become "visions," akin to the Apostle John's apocalyptic book of Revelation, in which the asylum's inmates, occupying seven cells, open windows to worlds and experiences parallel to theirs. These enactments comprise Hope's Dream-book.

The second and perhaps more crucial point is the iconoclastic significance that Harris interjects into the narrative through the relation. Their circumstances signify the breaking down of barriers, the rejection of stiff moral "standards" for a more passionate expression of love. In a quaint inversion of a biblical archetype, Hope and Butterfly revisit the story of the fall and, rather than see themselves as fallen Adam and Eve, feel empowered by their transgression while they view D'eath as the serpent to be outsmarted:

> Whatever kinship existed with outcast Adam and Eve, their unfinished genesis or inner bible was different. Theirs was not a state of exile from India or Europe or Africa or Palestine or Egypt or China or anywhere on the globe. Not exiles were they, but voyagers within and between all cultures, through and between all worlds. Theirs was a trespass backwards and forwards in time in the wake of a death-in-life strait-jacketed existence that still threatened their planet earth, still threatened to reduce their planet earth into becoming a mere pawn of linear inevitability, linear pollution. That parallel trespass illumined the ribs of space. (37)

Christopher D'eath is, by the very paradox of his naming, the quintessence of "death-in-life," a threat to the creative imagination, the coital exuberance that floods the consciousness of the "redeemed" biblical archetypes. In them, we recognize, again, the persistent philosophical argument of Harris that calls for a dismantling of all forms of monolithic philosophies and a search for meanings in parallel existences and multidimensional spheres.

Harris's quest for meaning through the prism of various life forms affects the manner in which he views the immediate material environment. In his artistic world, nothing is ordinary; the interconnections between the animate and the inanimate, the parallel worlds that make up the "Constellation of Tiresias," are too tangible to be erased by an imagination that insists on rigid categorizations. Thus, for Harris, enchantment becomes a critical device for the apprehension of reality; it is in the intensification of perception that a larger and more complex dimension of the image supersedes the primary one. We may categorize this metasensory apprehension as "magical," but that does not adequately represent it as a special paradigm in which the imagination captures parallel worlds. This paradigm shift is represented in *Resurrection* by the miracle staff that Daemon hands over to her grandmother as an initiation gesture when she assumes the role of Tiresias, the seer. In giving her the serpent staff, Daemon tells her, "You need a dead stick that is a serpent . . . Accept the impossible. Have faith . . . Faith in the metamorphoses of art" (8). In the mythic precedent, it was the staff, ordinary as it seemed, that metamorphosed to life's male and female essences when the blind seer struck it at seven-year intervals to the ground.[9]

In Hope's mythic text, the miracle staff is the agent that enables the characters to move in various bodies through various spaces. One such metamorphosis occurs when the hunting D'eath nearly catches Hope and Butterfly as they share a stolen moment in the forest. Butterfly dreams that they have been transformed into clear, glasslike beings on crystal water so transparent that they are rendered invisible to the eyes of D'eath, who approaches where they are in the trail of wild game. However, it is not a dream, for D'eath does come upon them. Further sublimated, the lovers leave D'eath with a troubled sense of something unusual occurring in space: "D'eath had paused nevertheless as if conscious of invisible movement, congealed energies, slow-motion lightning limbs waiting to fly. The thought brushed his mind (even as he suppressed it) that panic-stricken human flight up into space might offer a clue to congealed energies— scarcely understood (in a state of eclipse)—around which angels danced on the head of a pin-point constellation, in the womb of space" (63). At this critical moment, D'eath is capable of entering the other space where the lovers are but does not (the suppression of the thought suggests this); instead, he is grounded by his "earthly pursuits." He steps on Hope, who is invisible to him but nevertheless feels the pain of D'eath's movement. Once the danger is over as D'eath walks away from the scene, the couple takes flight. This is how the narrator presents it:

> Butterfly and Hope shot up. Bolt upright over Glass. Congealed yet eruptive energies of flight gripped them. They were fused by a transference of psyche, inanimate psyche (so to speak) into the animation of slow-motion lightning limbs. They had been mere things when D'eath trod upon an invisible bone in a mirror or upon a dry branch or dry leaf. But those "mere things" had sparked all over again a bridge in a storm and a descent into twilight. Now they sparked flight as if a numinous seed began to sprout wings, winged feet, winged dance. (64)

The most striking aspect of this passage is the accuracy of D'eath's earlier speculation on what could be happening at the crystal glass where he had stopped to look at his reflection. He had perceived other "energies"—resurrection energies—that his D['']eath personality could not interpret and which had become a potent agent for the survival of the secret lovers. They had stuck to the solidity of their bodies while surrendering to a psychic consciousness through which they escaped their adversary. As stated earlier, the magicality of the moment is less important than Harris's deeper aesthetic and philosophical statement by demanding that the reader attempt an adequate "leap of faith" (where all things are possible) and perceive the parallel worlds in which his characters exist.

Central to the apprehension of the matrix of worlds in *Resurrection* is an understanding of the relationship between memory and the imagination. In a nonlinear or nonspatialized time scheme, memory is not constructed as the recollected narrative gleaned from a past. There is no temporal demarcation between that past per se and the consciousness of the present. Memory is more a restoration of what has always been than a recollection of what had been. The restoration can take the form of a dream, a cinematic representation, or simply an enactment by characters existing in the present. For example, Hope's Dream-book is not actually a narrative of concluded action; the novel suggests that he is in the process of writing it, and he summons the inmates of "The Asylum for the Greats" to "feature" in it. They are inmates whose lives begin ordinarily but who easily wear the mask of other personages in the theater of world history—a "concert of transfigured opposition between the dead and the living, between ghost and solidity" (156).

Take the figure of one of the inmates, Monty the Venezuelan. He escapes from a trial for stabbing a drunken miner—he insists he is innocent—by enacting a fake death in which the people and police give him up as having drowned in one of the rapids in Sorrow Hill. Through this contrived symbolic death, dislocated as he is, Monty ends up in the asylum where he claims to be Montezuma, the legendary Aztec emperor. Monty's consciousness continues to vacillate between the events leading to his arrival at the asylum and a total evocation of Montezuma. The latter proves very significant, for when the mask of Montezuma takes control, the narrative revisits the history of the fall of the great Aztec civilization at the onslaught of the ruthless European conquistadors. The deposed emperor appears in the asylum seeking revenge.

Unfortunate as the fall of the ancient empire is, vengeance has no place in the Dream-book Hope is writing, for "Conquest had engineered, an appetite for revenge which had disfigured, and was disfiguring, so many landscapes, so many villages, so many cities, around the globe. From the Lebanon to Somalia, from Port-au-Prince to Soweto, from Sorrow Hill to Peru" (92–93). Montezuma may not have his revenge, but through Hope's Dream-book, this historic figure's life and times resonate and are interrogated in the present.

Montezuma's appearance in Hope's narrative does not merely make a statement about the horror of vengeance; his appearance deals more with the imaginative evocation of a moment in history as a means of making sense of that moment and pointing out its implications for the future and the present. The "madness" that possesses Monty/Montezuma is such that implicates all parties involved in the making of Sorrow Hill, of the New World. Between the oppressive and exploitative activities of the conquistadors and the autocratic and vindictive regime of the deposed emperor, there is equal condemnation. The New World is a metaphor for displacement, both for the colonizer and the colonized, and only a new historical consciousness can effect a resolution. As Hope writes in his letter to Montezuma, "You had been dismembered . . . within the gateway of the New World. Where there is dismemberment there is the creative necessity to visualize re-memberment. *That* is the paradox of the New World and if we fail to understand it conflicting hordes will prey upon us" (102). I consider the term "re-memberment" most definitive of Harris's notion of the conceptualization of memory and imagination. What is called for is a restoration of what has always been a *member* of a whole.

Furthermore, dreams serve as agents of re-membering. Indeed, there is a relationship between the way dreams feature in Hope's book and the nature of the asylum inmates' "insanity." The inmates do not only recall the circumstances leading to their arrival at the asylum; they also imaginatively reconstruct personalities historically dated to the past—from Socrates to the Egyptian king Akhenaton to the biblical Judas the betrayer to Leonardo da Vinci and to Montezuma—and open up a new space to interrogate their lives and what they represent. Through the mediation of Hope, described as the "Supreme agent of Jest" who "frequently echoed the independent thoughts of his characters" (125);[10] Judge, the dumb sage at Sorrow Hill who is Daemon's uncle; and Daemon, the doctor in charge of the asylum, the reappearances are constantly evoked in present time. The constructive and sometimes disturbing reality of these evocations becomes one of the critical issues of the novel. As each of the seven "books" of the novel focuses on one or two inmates, Hope and Daemon raise the question of what is insanity.

Disillusioned by the failed vision of a liberation movement he had sympathies for, Len, a physics and chemistry professor at a Brazilian university, escapes from his homeland to settle in Sorrow Hill as a messenger in the Bank of El Dorado. Len executes a spectacular robbery of the bank in which he fools the entire establishment into seeing the operation as one huge Hollywood cinematic production. Meanwhile, he gets away with half a million Guyanese dollars and some gold and diamonds. The police are unable to solve the mystery of the robbery, but seven days later, Len confesses that he is the perpetrator. The entire community is scandalized by the confession, and though they follow him to his house and find the loot scattered all over the floor, they still do not believe he is the criminal they are seeking. In fact, his confession is so unbelievable to them that they dismiss him as having gone mad. But as he tells Hope in the asylum, his return is to "provide another unexpected angle upon sanity as a rare disease" (122) or perhaps to draw our attention to the idea of *in*sanity. Underlying Hope's book project, and, by extension, Harris's, is an interrogation of society's definition of in/sanity.

There is a possible dialogue between *Resurrection* and Michel Foucault's positions in *Madness and Civilization*. Foucault reveals that, from medieval times, madness has been a socially constructed condition, the society's apparatus for containing its members whose apprehension of their unconscious reality poses a threat to "reason." Understanding this dynamic, Foucault argues that what is called madness is, rather, "unreason." The key to understanding it is in dreams, which Foucault sees as the "language of madness" (101). The difference between reason and unreason is a question of what the dreamer, on waking up, makes of the reality experienced in sleep. This reality, Foucault argues, is not "erroneous"; it simply operates on a different logic. No wonder, then, that in *Resurrection* the figure Dream appears at the asylum, and the critical question he poses to June, one of the characters in the asylum, is "What is sanity? What is madness?" (156). In Harris's novel, the asylum, symbolically named Asylum for the Greats, which is a space set up to tactfully reduce inmates to nothingness, becomes a viable space for appraising the history of South America in relation to the world, "For the book [Hope's Dream book] interrogated itself to reflect the way the inmates of the asylum interrogated themselves, the way they were creating a theatre that questioned itself. And—as they did so—the characters in legend and history that the inmates claimed to be interrogated the age in which Hope lived. Even as Hope interrogated the age in which they lived, and was interrogated in turn" (178).

At first reading of the novel, it appears that Harris valorizes the written word over the oral. The indicators signal at every turn of the text: an author who edits another author's work; a narrator who constructs his narrative on the idea of a book project; the letters through which some of the characters address the reader to explain the significance of what has transpired; the character named Nameless who claims to be Socrates and avows to *inscribe* himself into the *pages* of the world (171); character names that derive their symbolism from idiosyncratic spellings; and so on. There is a definite recognition given to writing as not just a scribal activity but as an inherently conditioned agency for the conceptualization and articulation of deep philosophical notions. Yet Harris's use of the written word becomes subversive when his narrative calls attention to the oral tradition. The association is captured in the South American Arawak legend of Timehri, which Harris, in one of the novel's epigraphs, describes as the "hand of God that writes upon rocks and landscapes. It is also the hand of numinous Shadow that paints the stars in the rivers then washes them away." Timehri embodies both the scribal (visible) and nonscribal ("shadow") elements of the artist's imagination. Pointing out the significance of Timehri in the works of Harris and Aubrey Williams, Kamau Brathwaite sees the use of the legend as the Caribbean writer's path to "discovering word for object, image for the Word" (350). In the novel, Timehri appears in the sequences of dreams in which the characters transfigure into other bodies and spaces.

Another pertinent aspect of the oral-written interface in the novel comes through Hope's description of one of his masking devices, the "Ventriloquism of Spirit." As shown above, most of the narrative action in the novel takes place through the characters' ability to speak for others in their own voices. The dead, dumb as it were, still speak through the asylum inmates. Judge, a prophetic figure in Sorrow Hill, embodies this principle. He is dumb, but Hope is his agent for imparting wisdom and meaning to the lives and experiences of the community: the intangible Word, to which Timehri's scribal hand gives life. Hope explicates this paradoxical relationship between the spoken and the written when he addresses Judge in the asylum: "I take my cue from you, Judge, from your mask that I visualize acutely as I write, from your dumb being which speaks to me from the *silent* pages of my book. My book is silent. . . . It is as dumb as you. You speak! It speaks! You are silent, dumb. It is silent, dumb" (53; emphasis in original). Thus, the artist's imagination, following Harris's portrayal, is such that it lends itself to the recapturing of essences drawn from the mystery of the word. In *Resurrection,* Hope is the chief ventriloquist.

Conscious of how dominant political powers use orality and literacy to create a literary hierarchy whereby spoken art (which seems to still thrive in less developed countries) is subordinated by writing in more developed societies, Harris deconstructs the logic of such hierarchization. His construct of il/literacy, as earlier noted, does not depend on just the ability to read and write. In *Resurrection,* he evokes again the "literacy of the Imagination" (10) idea. While literacy has always been defined in scribal terms—that is, the ability to read what is written or to write—and mostly through the philosophical framework of the conquistador, Harris centers literacy on knowledge, the kind of knowledge Hope and the characters in the Dream-book possess. It is the power of the imagination to transcend the limitations of spatial time and understand the interconnections existing among lives, continents, cultures, and beliefs, and between animate and inanimate beings. That part of the Western tradition that historically has resisted this view either through its insistence on monolithic systems or through the ideology that framed slavery, colonialism, and imperialism is in this Harrisian construct "illiterate."

The implications are not lost on the blind seer Tiresias, Doctor Daemon's grandmother, for she ponders in Hope's book, "Was terrifying literacy, terrifying insight into the malaise of a civilization, a kind of madness in an illiterate world? Is literacy the burning tongue of a god that visits dimensions and places of history where men and women surrender to fortresses of ignorance?" (10). Hope and the occupants of the seven dream cells in the asylum are all natives of South America—Guyana, Puerto Rico, Brazil, Venezuela, and so on. They come from a region that historically has been a site for unprecedented capitalist pillaging and exploitation, human oppression, and environmental abuse. It is in this environment, the Sorrow Hill of world history, that Harris evokes Resurrection planet, another space similar to the Palace of the Peacock in Harris's debut novel where hope exists based on the community's literacy of the imagination. At the end of the novel, Hope, donning the mask of Archangel, leaves a parting charge to the reader that reveals the full significance of Sorrow Hill and his Dream-book. It is so critical that the words are capitalized:

CREATE A SPACE WITHIN THE COMPACT SINS OF AN ECONOMY OF GUILT, AN ECONOMY OF GREED. THE MAD ONES—WHO SEEK TO COMMAND NO ONE—WHO BEAR THE EXTREMITIES OF THE ILLNESSES OF CONQUISTADORIAL CIVILIZATIONS—ARE THE RARE SIN EATERS OF HISTORY. . . . IN THE MIRROR OF THE SPACE AGE HANGS AN INNER SPACE AND ITS SLOW AND MEASURELESS BREACH IN THE TYRANNIES OF MATERIALIST ARCHETYPES. (242)

Reenacting History in Anansi's Tangled Web

Jonestown is no doubt an effort to present, on a grand scale, the fate of the "mad ones," the victims of ruthless capitalist hegemony. Almost two decades after an American cult leader, James Warren Jones (a.k.a. Jim Jones), leads his congregation to a mass suicide in his large secluded property in Guyana, Harris revisits the dark event to reveal how it fits into a larger narrative of imperialism and capitalist exploitation. *Jonestown* shares some affinities with the previous work, *Resurrection at Sorrow Hill.* In both narratives, Harris abdicates the privileged position of "author." He is instead an editor while the owner of the "manuscript," Francisco Bone, the sole survivor of the mass suicide that he calls the "Day of the Dead" (3), is the pseudonym of the author. *Jonestown,* however, begins with a cover letter from Bone to "W. H." stating the purpose of his writing to the editor whom he understands has "sympathies for voyagers of the Imagination" (3).[11] The authors of both novels experience similar degrees of dislocated consciousness, which explains why they both consider their works "Dream-books."

If the narrative strategy in *Jonestown* is a rehash of his previous works, it is exactly as Harris would have it. The title of one of his previous novels, *The Infinite Rehearsal,* aptly captures the novelist's argument that human history is a continuous rehearsal without resolution; art equally subsists on this principle by continually revisiting trodden territories, with each revisitation throwing more light on what has always been there. Al Creighton, however, amplifies the significance of rehearsal by seeing it as "man's very purgatorial path to salvation" through a process "involving several changing masks of carnival" (199). In *Jonestown,* Harris ventures further in his exploration of the concept "fiction of reality." It is not just that the fictive character, Francisco Bone, writes asking Harris to edit his manuscript; the central event that forms the body of the Dream-book is a historically verifiable event. The Guyanese tragedy did take place, and, incidentally, the weekly news magazine *Time* reported one survivor, Grover Davis, age seventy-nine, who jumped into a ditch and played dead when Jones ordered the congregation to drink the cyanide-laced Fla-vor-Aid.[12] In *Jonestown,* Bone is the lone survivor of the disaster. He hides away at the critical moment. However, these are as far as historical affinities go; the Guyanese tragedy operates in Harris's imagination as part of a complex theatrical plot that resonates with global and philosophical implications.

Sixteen years after his near-death experience in Jonestown, and traumatized by the experience, Bone begins a series of recollections about that day and what led to it. His recollections assume mythic significance as he begins his narrative caught in a position remarkably similar to the biblical figure, Jacob:[13] "I lay in a clump of bushes like a dead man. . . . My head rested on a cushion of stone. I dreamt of angels ascending and descending into Jonestown. . . . How incredibly soft is stone when one fears flesh-and-blood!" (13). Jacob had robbed his brother, Esau, of their father's blessing and was fleeing from his bitter brother; for his part, Bone reneges on a pact he made with his associates, Jones and Deacon, by refusing to die voluntarily. In this narrative, the dream is most important. As noted earlier, dreams constitute the medium of transmitting the complex and broader dimensions of reality. For Bone, the dream is the reason for, and content of, his Dream-book; as Mageye, his childhood teacher and guide, tells him, the dreamer is the "surrogate creator of all systems and universes" (211). Mageye's statement points to the enormous potentiality Harris affords his dream narratives. The combination of the conscious, the unconscious, and the subconscious creates new dimensions for defining and apprehending reality, unlike the narrow prescription of the conscious as the only window for perceiving reality.[14]

Reality in Harrisian terms is constructed within a different cosmic frame. Time and space transcend the temporal as Harris favors a "different topography or map of Imagination that breaches the human-centred cosmos" (6). Narrative time is patterned on ancient Maya and African conceptualizations of time. The intricate link among the dead, the unborn, and the living ensures a continuum in the cycle of life. The dead are the ones who reemerge as the living; the unborn are the community's regenerative life force.[15] In this ontological frame, there is no spatialization of time. The "present" could be the affirmation of a "past," or a counterpoint. Events that mark a time line are in continuous cosmic motion that resists material division. In relation to narrative time, Bone tells W. H. in his letter:

> To sail back into the past is to come upon "pasts" that are "futures" to previous "pasts" which are "futures" in themselves to prior "pasts" *ad infinitum*. There is no absolute beginning, for each "beginning" comes after an unwritten past that awaits a new language. What lies behind us is linked incalculably to what lies ahead of us in that the future is a sliding scale backwards into the unfathomable past within the Virgin womb of time. (5)

It is necessary to stress the place of language in the construction of this narrative time and, by implication, reality. Language is the powerful agent that transports the text of a past into the present. The past is unwritten because the language of its text is always in the process of discovery. It is the language of dream. Through this language, a synthesis of parallel spaces and worlds occurs. Bone puts this point across more elegantly when he remarks in his Dream-book, "The surrender of frames to inner frames and still inner frames—in plumbing the illumination of the innermost Word—is the music and the variable orchestra of reality" (208). Dream makes possible the *re*-presentation of what is familiar in new light. The reconstituted reality does not replace the old one but expands its dimensions.

By surrendering itself to "the variable orchestra of reality," Bone's Dream-book is also able to advance a different narrative aesthetic. The plot structure is not merely convoluted but driven by the parallel and sometimes simultaneous existences of individual characters in different times. This is Harris's way of revealing the inadequacy of conventional narrative forms to plumb the complex psyche of his characters; their existences conjured as fantasies, dreams, and physical encounters demand a more expansive ontological canvas. Indeed, in the same interview with Fred D'Aguiar, Harris explains the reason behind the multiple lives of his characters. Asked why Donne, the horseman in *Palace of the Peacock,* is shot and hangs in the air simultaneously and is later depicted as drowning in his first life, Harris replies,

> This is important as it brings into play three lives he could have lived and which fiction should explore. I know that the view of science tends to be that we are all genetically coded, but I would suggest interior lives that touch nature and make us into *living* sculptures. Freedom therefore needs to be explored in depths beyond conventional linearities. A sculpture appears inanimate, ornamental, in its fixed lines, but it may have a psychical momentum within its stillness that makes it a piece of *living* art. Can a sculpture encompass the whole life or the whole death it presents? Would there not have to be "second deaths" and "second lives" in a fiction that seeks a wholeness beyond the violence that seems the inevitable and apparently absolute frame of human existence? (77; emphasis in original)

Similarly, the search for wholeness in the Jonestown tragedy leads Bone to multiple existences derived from Mayan, African, and European belief systems and mythologies. His Dream-book is "memory theatre fictionality," "a net of associations of 'pasts' and 'presents' and 'futures' in which one could trace an immense and subtle transference of Masks such as [he] had glimpsed in the Nether World, in Limbo Land, in the Cave of the Moon, and elsewhere, in the aisle or street beneath the window of the cell" (76). Franscisco's branding of his writing as "memory theatre fictionality" redefines conventional fiction. For one, the emphasis on memory and theater celebrates fiction as simultaneously a highly ritualized contrivance (theater) and an entity existing on its own and embodying events locatable in various existential spaces (memory). This is the form of fiction that can possibly accommodate the fractal Caribbean history and experience, the kind that is, in Bone's words, "wholly different . . . from conventional European fiction, an epic net conversant with the European Conquest of the ancient Americas but antecedent to European models" (76). By implication, the Dream-book as constituted in Harris's language and extensive cross-cultural mythologies is also a reconceptualization of fiction so that the postcolonial subject may find a new space and language to counter the colonizer's paradigm.

In *Jonestown,* dream is performative. Bone escapes death at the hands of Jonah Jones but travels back in time to his childhood village Albuoystown, where he meets his grade school teacher Mr. Mageye. He must reexperience the critical events of that past, simultaneously feeling the anxiety or innocence of the moment and possessing knowledge of the implications of that moment from having experienced it in the future. In addition to role-playing, Bone meets his twin-skeleton, who reminds him, "Memory is archetypal. It is shared between fleshed Bone and twin-Skeleton" (110). There is the obvious pun on Bone's surname, but the appearance of the skeleton who could be regarded as the archetype of history is intended to remind Bone that what has happened to him in the future (the Jonestown tragedy), from which he is retreating into his past, requires that he see himself as a figure playing in a repetitive text. Bone survives the massacre; his twin-skeleton does not. Rather, the twin-skeleton descends into hell to experience the pain of having collaborated with Jones in the grand deceit and exploitation of the people of Jonestown as his "left-hand man" (82).

Furthermore, Mageye the schoolteacher, whom Bone describes as his "Magus-Jester of History" (35), like Everyman Masters in *Carnival,* is the guide to this past. He is both a seer and an actor, and Bone's journeys through time consist of encounters with archetypes that perform in what the book calls "Memory theatre." As a seer, Mageye imbues his pupil with a recreative force symbolized by the "Lazarus arm" with which he will later preach love and resurrection to a chaotic world.[16] Mageye also commands his student to put on masks to emphasize the significance of the voyages as an elaborate carnival. Naming follows this carnival tradition—Carnival Lord Death, Prisoner, Predator, Pig, and others. Each character-figure role-plays its name.[17]

Jonestown presents one of Harris's most critical interrogations of the survival of the folkloric tradition that both the enslaved Africans and the indentured Indians brought to the New World. The secular African trickster figure Ananse; his mythic counterpart, Eshu or Legba; and Kali, the many-armed Indian virgin goddess, all come under scrutiny as the novelist searches for their relevance in twentieth-century South American life.

Harris interprets the relationship between the white American Jonah Jones and his black lieutenants Deacon and Bone as a manifestation of the disuse or dysfunction that has befallen the folkloric characters. Jones's retreat from his country to the jungles of Guyana, where he builds Jonestown with the collaboration of Deacon and Bone, raises the specter of ideological pollution, which hegemonic Euro-American states inflict on nations such as Guyana. The recruitment of the two lieutenants with whom he ostensibly wanted to "build a new Rome in the South American rain forest within the hidden flexibilities of civilizations that had collapsed in the past" (126) marks a dangerous development that the novel dramatizes as having fatal consequences. Ananse (Bone), the spinner of webs of intrigue and survivor of the trauma of the Middle Passage, compromises his survival secret by entering into league with his enslaver.

Jones's foray into the South American jungle is portrayed as a dubious move by a power-wielding West to control and destroy the potency of a cultural tradition that has survived years of brutality and exploitation, and which, therefore, by its resilience, exposes the hollowness of the touted supremacy of the Western tradition. The latter is a consciousness that is still illiterate in imagination, despite its literacy in the common application of the term. Jonah Jones entices his associates with hopes of an empire in the heart of South America, but the text also exposes him as a patron of whores and an American bank fraud. Deacon, the "fallen angel," returns to the region only to betray the trust of the dream community of Roraima (after being shown the sacred secrets of the land) by running away with precious stones from the sacred rock. He, too, has exploitative sexual liaisons with the women of the community.

Mageye's magic camera reveals the truth of Jonah Jones's real mission, creating a cinema of ghosts of the past in dialogue with their actions. As the dead Jonah appears in the theater of Bone's memory, he confesses to what has driven him to build Jonestown and why he recruits Bone and Deacon. Significantly, he articulates his action through the Ananse idiom: "When Anansi becomes as much a ruling appetite . . . as the former missionary or ruler or master with whom he contended—then the establishment and the trickster are equals" (201–2). However, the promise of equality is flawed; equality occurs only at death, on the Day of the Dead. Even this instance is invalidated by Jones's absolute power over Jonestown, demonstrated by the unilateral decision. He says, "I shall persuade my people here in Jonestown to eat or drink whatever I dish out. Poison is palatable when it is braced with projected dominion over all species in a coming paradise or eternity. . . . It's not just cyanide in Coca-Cola. . . . It's the conquest of the lower orders"

(203). Does a seemingly simple folkloric tradition carry a heavier burden of a sophisticated international political agenda of domination and extermination based on racial superiority?

Bone wears the mask of Deacon, as his teacher continues to show the film of their life. The use of the mask at this point is twofold. On the one hand, he retains the consciousness of his dead associate so that Jonah's deceit can be exposed. On the other, Mageye imbues him with a double vision so that not only is he able to interact with the numerous frames of memory theater, but he also receives the truth or significance of each frame in deeper and broader terms. For example, as Jones reveals the ramifications of Ananse in his Jonestown plot, Bone, wearing the mask of Deacon, recognizes Deacon's and his own complicity in the tragedy. They knew of Jones's ultimate intention but simply did not warn their people. They have lived a lie, even though it is Deacon and Bone, in the latter's dream, who kill Jones in revenge on the Day of the Dead.

By making Deacon and Bone partially responsible for the outcome of Jonestown, Harris opens the way for reconciliation. His mission is to indict the Western expansionist project in the so-called Third World countries, as much as it is to expose the culpability of the elite in those countries.[18] Harris's vision attempts to transcend the temptations of simple racial or political grandstanding; his novels make a compelling argument that humanity's failing through history is a consequence of an illiteracy of the imagination. The fixation with unyielding boundaries and the refusal to apprehend reality as a construct of parallel spaces and cross-cultural traditions are manifestations of this illiteracy. It is no wonder that, in Harris's fictive-realist enactment, most of the world's dark moments—slavery, colonialism, mass killings, the Inquisition—have been perpetrated by societies driven by a monolithic perspective blind to the mystery of reality.

In *The Womb of Space*, Harris states what one may describe as his literary manifesto thus:

> The basis of our inquiry lies in the conception that one may address oneself to diverse fictions and poetries as if they are the art of a universal genius hidden everywhere in dual rather than monolithic presence, in the mystery of innovative imagination that transforms concepts of mutuality and unity, and which needs to appear in ceaseless dialogue between cultures if it is to turn away from a world habituated to the pre-emptive strike of conquistadorial ego. (137)

Certainly, the novels examined here are efforts at participating in that dialogue. Harris pays a distinct homage to his combined African, Native American, Mayan, and European mythic traditions, even as I have emphasized the folkloric imagination as a dominant strand. Considering the scribal medium in which Harris works, the folkloric aesthetic is more implicit than overt. The African mask motif, for instance, is essential to the character role-playing prevalent in his narratives. The mask is both a spectacle in itself and a medium that allows the performer to appropriate the attributes and consciousness of the masked figure. Transformation occurs, releasing the imagination to a world of wonder and limitless possibilities.

Harris uses the carnival idiom to reveal the limitations of European paradigms. The identification of literacy, not with the ability to read and write but with the ability to grasp the paradoxes of existence, is part of his "continuing analysis of the incisive principles and values of the cross-cultural imagination" (Hamlet 207). Harris's notion of alchemy enables him to retrieve mythic figures from the Old World—African and European—and refashion them into the image of the Caribbean. Alchemy is not to prefer one to the other but "to include [both] within newly inclusive and tolerant wholes" (Williams and Riach 60). In this framework, there are no rigid distinctions. It is as fluid as the white Jonah Jones wearing the mask of the African Ananse or Len, the Brazilian professor, wearing the Italian Leonardo da Vinci's mask in the asylum. Harris's works, Alan Riach suggests, belong to "the transgressive literature of empire," due to the power Harris confers on his characters, both the colonizer and the colonized, to reverse roles, to retain or abandon their positions (34).

In Harris's narratives, dream is the channel for grasping the mystery of reality. The mediumistic quality of dream as a literary device enables Harris's characters to move across spaces and travel through time. Moreover, dream is the language that continually regenerates reality. It is the language of enchantment in that it defamiliarizes what is ordinary and causes the reader to pause and engage the narrative from an entirely new perspective. In the same vein, Harris imbues his language with "strangeness" that requires a folkloric aesthetic approach of interpretation. Within the discourse of enchantment could be located new meanings that cloak old archetypes. His language calls attention to the folk tradition, and, in that space, what he writes becomes a voice that speaks against a formally literate world that seems to have forgotten its need to be first literate in the imagination.

– FOUR –

"Something to Figure In"

Toni Morrison and the Complexities
of Oral Narrativity

I started out believing that life was made just so the world would have some
way to think about itself, but that it had gone awry with humans because flesh,
pinioned by misery, hangs on to it with pleasure. Hangs on to wells and a boy's
golden hair; would just as soon inhale sweet fire caused by a burning girl as
hold a maybe-yes maybe-no hand. I don't believe that anymore. Something is
missing. Something rogue. Something else you have to figure in before you can
figure it out.

—Toni Morrison, *Jazz*

Toni Morrison is unarguably the most distinguished African American
novelist and, certainly, among the select group of influential American
writers of the twentieth century.[1] As the first African American recipient
of the Nobel Prize for literature in 1993, Morrison's literary stature looms
large over black literary production in the United States. And for good
reasons. Morrison's first novel, *The Bluest Eye,* poignantly captures the tragedy and fallacy of an American society that privileges one race over others. Her subsequent novels remain focused on the black experience within
the dominant white American society. Indeed, some critics have identified
three of her novels—*Beloved* (1987), *Jazz* (1992), and *Paradise* (1998) as a trilogy charting three key historical moments in African American history,
namely, slavery/reconstruction, the great northward migration, and post–
civil rights eras.[2] Nonetheless, Morrison's eight novels are profound for
their ability to weave historical relevance into highly gendered narratives.
Keen as she is in charting the inseparability of white American political
and cultural history from black America's,[3] Morrison's focus hardly leaves
the affairs of women and the men in their lives, making her novels a wide
canvas of diverse female characters. Although novels such as *Tar Baby* and

Love center on the lives of the black upper class, most of Morrison's novels deal with ordinary folks wrestling with demons in their past that seem to thwart their efforts at making sense of their present. In these enactments, Morrison infuses her stories with the kind of folk sensibility that grounds the works as decidedly African American.

I am particularly interested in Morrison's construction of memory as an oral or folkloric sign that illuminates her creative imagination etched in written form. Rather than define memory as an ordinary recall of event, which in itself may be said to be either "reliable" or not, Morrison politicizes the activity of memory by using it as the medium through which black experience can be represented. This is not all; fashioning a black voice, a voice that when it is represented in writing is subjected to spoken inflections, is also important to Morrison; it is yet another way by which she attempts to recreate the dual cultural heritage of blacks in the New World.

In my reading of *Song of Solomon, Jazz,* and *Paradise,* I suggest that these works are, more than other considerations, a verbal performance celebrating the black voice in print and a testament to the durability of the spoken word and other forms of oral tradition in preserving black history through racial memory. Morrison is conscious of the act of writing as a performance, and this is why she imbues her narrators and characters with a cadence of speech that suggests an oral artist who knows that, in addition to being entertained by what she says, the audience is also interested in how well she extends the possibilities of the community's linguistic and artistic resources.

In effect, the three novels under consideration will show that Morrison's narrative strategies are deeply embedded in the black literary tradition, both in the manner by which she chooses to historicize the black experience in the Americas and in her ardent efforts to represent this experience with a keen sense of the spoken or "talking" roots of the African American literary tradition.[4] Thus, when Herbert William Rice, for instance, while discussing *Song of Solomon,* states that "even a cursory glance at the novel demonstrates its links with mainstream American literature" (*Toni Morrison* 56), one must ask if the attention Morrison gives to memory, and to the validity of myth as an aspect of history, is part of the "mainstream" American narrative. This attempt to wrest Morrison's art from its oral-black roots and neutralize its ethnic heritage by submerging it in "mainstream" literature resonates with efforts to find Western influences for her writings. No doubt, artists can be compared with their peers; such a comparison raises suspicions, however, when the goal is to suggest that one cannot be significant without the other.[5] Morrison herself puts it this way: "Finding or imposing Western influences in/on Afro-American literature has value, but when its sole purpose is to *place* value only where that influence is located, it is pernicious" (emphasis in original). The danger, as she rightly points out, with such an approach to her work, or that of any African American, for that matter, is that it "may lead to an incipient orphanization of the work in order to issue its adoption papers" ("Unspeakable Things" 23). My reading of Morrison's novels recognizes their full rights as offspring of a vibrant black imaginative tradition and as conveyors of the African American reality in its complexity.[6]

In *Song of Solomon,* the history of the African American in the United States is one that can only be textualized through its "inscription" in the memory of the community. The oppressive role that illiteracy has played in understating, if not obliterating, the presence of the African American in American history provides the impetus for the novel's central event, which is the retrieval of the Dead's family genealogy from obscurity through a series of convoluted oral histories preserved in the memory of the community.

A clarification of the use of the term "memory" is necessary. Memory is part of what defines the human consciousness, and I do not wish to fetishize its presence in Morrison's narratives. To remember or to forget, Matthew Hugh Erdelyi writes, are the two "contradicting tendencies of memory" (15). For my present purpose, though, I find the French historian Pierre Nora's description of memory very useful, especially in the way he sets it off against history. "Memory is life, borne by living societies founded in its name," he argues, then continues: "It remains in permanent evolution, open to the dialectic of remembering and forgetting, unconscious of its successive deformations, vulnerable to manipulation and appropriation, susceptible to being long dormant and periodically revived." Conversely, history "is the reconstruction, always problematic and incomplete, of what is no longer" (285). The problem with history, one would surmise, is its need for exactitude ("reconstruction"), a need shunned by memory.

However, Nora complicates the difference between memory and history by arguing that in our modern times what we call memory is actually history. The kind of environment in which "real memory" operates—spontaneous and unself-conscious—has been dislodged, Nora states, "under the pressure of a fundamentally historical sensibility" (284). The emergence of several voices or groups, especially those hitherto silenced by hegemonic history, and the occurrence of radically transformative world events have created an age wherein what is remembered is not left to chance and spontaneity. The expression, "Never again," commonly tied to the Jewish Holocaust, for example, becomes an injunction for the group, indeed, the world, to etch this particular event in memory. What is remembered assumes orderliness and specificity that bring memory under the province of history. Thus, to use the Holocaust example, that singular historical event becomes a *"lieu de mémoire,"* a site of memory "where memory crystallizes and secretes itself . . . at a particular historical moment, a turning point where consciousness of a break with the past is bound up with the sense that memory has been torn—but torn in such a way as to pose the problem of the embodiment of memory in certain sites where a sense of historical continuity persists" (ibid.).

The Middle Passage and plantation slavery remains a traumatic historical event, which resonates in and influences African American political and cultural consciousness. The will to remember that period, especially when the ramifications of the experience still exist, constitutes black racial memory. What Morrison does is transform that memory into a literary metaphor that best conveys the unique position and experience of the African American. In this typology, memory is not an "art," as Frances A. Yates's *Art of Memory* suggests, but an eruptive force that the African American writer harnesses in order to present a counter-American narrative. In fact, it is more appropriate to refer to the kind of memory present in African American narratives as "counter-memory," which George Lipsitz defines as "look[ing] to the past for the hidden histories of those excluded from dominant narratives" (162).[7] Morrison's conceptualization of memory manifests in oral histories, that is, histories that her characters assume responsibility for telling, though the narratives collapse into one extended and convoluted narrative of the community. The disruptive effect of these histories on the American narrative is in part a direct consequence of their nonlinearity. In his study of social memory, Paul Connerton notes that oral histories by an oppressed group produce a different type of history that runs counter to the structure of the dominant narrative: "The oral history of subordinate groups will produce another type of history: one in which not only will most of the details be different, but in which the very construction of meaningful shapes will obey a different principle. Different details will emerge because they are inserted, as it were, into a different kind of narrative home" (19).

The narrative principle that informs Morrison's novels is oral and the stories she tells are so composed within a different frame of memory that her coinage, "rememory," which is featured significantly in *Beloved*, becomes a conscious attempt to distinguish her own construct. Sethe explains it to her daughter Denver as a phenomenon that has a life of its own outside of events, places, and people:

> Someday you be walking down the road and you hear something or see something going on. So clear. And you think it's you thinking it up. A thought picture. But no. It's when you bump into a rememory that belongs to somebody else. Where I was before I came here, that place is real. It's never going away. Even if the whole farm—every tree and grass blade of it dies. The picture is still there and what's more, if you go there—you who never was there—if you go there and stand in the place where it was, it will happen again; it will be there for you, waiting for you. (36)

Rememory becomes a present thought of a past, solidified in an image kept alive by its capacity to be evoked or reenacted by virtually any member of the community. Sethe's escape from Sweet Home does not exorcise the ghost of the harrowing life at the plantation—an experience that assumes a physicality by the appearance and return of Beloved. Together with Paul D, Sethe relives life at Sweet Home and rememory creates the impetus for living.[8]

In her essay "Memory, Creation and Writing," Morrison accentuates the act of memory as living tissue in the community's sense of being when she asserts that "memory (the deliberate act of remembering) is a form of willed creation. It is not an effort to find out the way it really was—that is research. The point is to dwell on the way it appeared and why it appeared in that particular way" (385). The statement points toward an important aspect of her conceptualization: remembering as a conscious act. To dwell on a past that the dominant narrative has tried to erase through contrived history is both an act of resistance and a process of communal validation. Thus, Aimable Twagilimana's statement that rememory is "an activation of the past, to the time of stories told by mothers and grandmothers, to the middle passage, and even to Africa, the land of origins" (103) proves a useful amplification of Morrison's position. For what she does is to establish rememory as the mediation between the oral storytelling practices of the ancestral land and New World black experience.

However, this mediation is not without its problems. While communal rememory empowers members of the community to preserve what they deem important to their well-being through folkloric agencies, rememory in itself does not legitimize all practices or ideas that spring from the oral process. The three novels are important for how they showcase

Morrison's representation of oral traditional arts in complex ways. In the novels, memory operates both as a counternarrative discourse against a dominant and literacy-biased history and as the agency through which oral forms of group identity are celebrated. But these novels also reveal Morrison's interrogation of the politics behind the performance of oral traditional arts in the African American community.

Resurrecting the Song of the Deads

Caught between the contradicting threads of a family history as recounted by his parents, Milkman Dead comes to the realization that he must take personal responsibility for reconciling the histories through a journey back to his roots. He is aware that the circumstances of his own birth are the main cause of estrangement between his parents, hence the necessity for his journey. Though his father, Macon Dead, does not have doubts that he is Milkman's biological father, he cannot but be suspicious of the unusual nickname, Milkman, his son acquired, which, to him, "sounded dirty, intimate, and hot" (15). His wife, Ruth, on the other hand, struggles to supplant an ambiguously incestuous relationship she had with her late father and the sexually sterile relationship with her husband by maintaining an apparently erotic breast-feeding attachment to young Milkman. Confused by a web of contending family relationships, Milkman tells his older friend Guitar, "Everybody wants something from me. . . . Something they think I got. I don't know what it is—I mean what it is they really want." His friend ominously replies, "They want your life, man," and further clarifies his statement, "It is the condition our condition is in. Everybody wants the life of the black man. Everybody" (222). Later, Guitar's words resonate in his consciousness as he watches the men in the hunting party skin and divide portions of the bobcat killed during the night's expedition. As Luther, one of the men, begins cleaning out the animal's entrails, Milkman asks him what he is going to do with them since they obviously have enough of the better portions of the game. Luther roundly replies, "Eat him!" (283). It is at this moment that Guitar's words assume a physical immediacy, for just as the men appropriate every part of the animal—down to its entrails—so is his own being, his entire self, sought by opposing forces. He must break the viciousness of the quest by reconstructing his past in order to take full control of his self. It is important to stress Milkman's journey of self-discovery; some have argued that it is his materialism represented by the search for the bag of gold at the cave that motivates Milkman's journey from Michigan to the Deep South; that is indeed the immediate reason, but the novel ultimately suggests that Milkman sees the journey as an opportunity to make sense of the chaotic present through the mediation of a hitherto curious and mythic past.[9]

In *Song of Solomon*, history is embodied in the people's consciousness. The community's consciousness embeds what it deems relevant through a process that defies rigid structures of documentation. This defiance erupts early in the novel at the impasse between the colored people and white council officials over the naming of a street where the city's only black medical doctor, Milkman's maternal grandfather, had lived. To the folks, it is "Doctor Street," while the city government officially lists the street as "Mains Avenue"—a name that, by its striking generic character, obliterates the value of the story connected with it. The people ignore such slanting of history and take recourse to naming it "Not Doctor Street," thereby solidifying through naming what their communal memory testifies (4). The name "Not Doctor Street" is a pithy account of both the government's attempt to impose an identity that bears no relation to the community's sense of historical relevance and the people's resistance to such an imposition. In addition, the narrator makes it clear that the people's naming preference is more powerful than all the city government's efforts to impose its preferred name.

Apart from the people's resolve to inscribe their folk values in the street's name, this opening incident foregrounds Morrison's notion of history and its construction among a marginalized group. The residents of Not Doctor Street constitute a community that must construct an alternative apparatus of history in order to validate their lives. The organs of the hegemony—the post office and the legislature—which exercise the privilege of conferring names and classifying city "landmarks" try unsuccessfully to erase the community's memories through a pathetically pedantic written memo. Interestingly, this approach of wielding literacy as power assumes an ironic twist in another naming "war" on a smaller scale that breaks out early on as well. Macon opens his realty office on Not Doctor Street and wants to erase "Sonny's Shop," the name of the previous occupant of the office space, by attempting to scrape the name off the glass window and replace it with a bland "OFFICE" sign. The narrator comments on the effort thus: "Scraping the previous owner's name was hardly worth the trouble since he couldn't scrape it from anybody's mind. His [Macon's] storefront office was never called anything but Sonny's Shop, although nobody now could remember thirty years back, when, presumably, Sonny did something or other there" (17). Macon, an entrepreneur driven by a materialistic passion to "own things [and things that] own other things" (55), attempts to literally paint over the community's memory with claims to a privileged space acquired through economic affluence. However, they resist him by maintaining the old name that, hazy as the facts associated with it may be in their memory, retains a relevance to their sense of community.

Through the portraits of the principal characters in the novel, a characterization of history as a composite of different strands of narrative performance within the community emerges. Pilate, Macon's only sister, for example, possesses mythic attributes because of having practically birthed herself and having no navel. Unlike her brother, whose obsession with wealth and desire to rub shoulders with the white propertied class alienates him from the rest of the black community, Pilate shuns materialism and is imbued with folk wisdom and knowledge of traditional healing arts. Interestingly, she secretly supplies Macon's wife, Ruth, with herbs with which Ruth is able to conceive Milkman, making Pilate Milkman's symbolic mother.

Although Pilate's unorthodox lifestyle, folk wisdom, and dogged individualism are highly celebrated in the narrative, her character alone nevertheless cannot sustain the weighty task of conveying the life force of the community's history. Her individual story overlaps with Ruth's and Macon's to give Milkman the full picture of his seemingly dysfunctional family. But the novel invests in Milkman's journey toward the ultimate retrieval and solidification of group identity through folklore. By the time Milkman finally unravels the mystery of the green bag Pilate has been carrying through all her life's journeys; the full text of the song we first heard from Pilate at the scene of insurance agent Smith's suicide flight; and the fascinating story of Solomon, Jake, and Sing, we realize how far Pilate's account is from a history that has been preserved in Shalimar's communal memory. Pilate weaves a history in which she is central. Though she is the one who goes back to the cave to gather the bones she believes belong to the white man her brother killed, in obedience to her dead father's instruction, and even though she is contrasted with her brother's material greed and craving for social recognition and influence, the history she narrates to Ruth, her (Pilate's) children, and her nephew remains individualistic, as individualistic as her brother's, Ruth's, and Guitar's. It is no wonder that, at the end, the narrative reveals that she has been carrying the wrong bones (even if they end up being her father's) and that she has woven an odyssey full of inconsistencies (257–58).[10]

On the other hand, Morrison presents history as a living construct etched in the consciousness of a community, preserved and transmitted through a collaborative performance by the group whose existence it validates. When Milkman arrives at Danville and introduces himself to the Reverend Cooper as Macon Dead's grandson, the clergyman replies excitedly, "I know your *people!*" (229; emphasis added). Milkman immediately recognizes the significance of the nominal change: "links," he calls it. Later, a group of old men who learn of Macon Dead's grandson's arrival gathers in Cooper's house, and what follows is a scene that aptly captures the novel's representation of black oral narrative performance:

> The more the old men talked—the more he [Milkman] heard about the only farm in the county that grew peaches, real peaches like they had in Georgia, the feasts they had when hunting was over, the pork kills in the winter and the work, the backbreaking work of a going farm—the more he missed something in his life. They talked about digging a well, fashioning traps, felling trees, warming orchards with fire when spring weather was bad, breaking young horses, training dogs. And in it all was his own father, the second Macon Dead, their contemporary, who was strong as an ox, could ride bareback and barefoot, who, they agreed, outran, outplowed, outshot, outpicked, outrode them all. (234)

In addition to depicting the making of history, the celebratory scene also affirms their survival as a community. The life story of Macon Dead and his son, in all its legendary proportions, is but a piece of narrative woven within the fabric of the larger history. Milkman is "the ignition that gunned their memories" (235), a catalyst that triggers the recapitulation of history for the invigoration of a dream in the community. The encomium they pour on the memory of Macon Dead reflects their own construct of a past; such a tribute is valued even more against the backdrop of the injustices perpetrated against them by the racist white majority. The story of Macon Dead, a fellow black man whose nominal identity is radically changed by his inability to read but who triumphs over the disadvantage and dies defending his property against vicious and jealous white neighbors, is no longer his history but their history, and the appropriation is represented by the conviviality of its performance. History is what is remembered and performed in verbal acts, and on each occasion of its recall it validates the lives of its performers.

Song of Solomon presents an American society that has politicized literacy by using it as an oppressive tool against African Americans. White slave owners strongly discouraged the slaves from learning to read and write, and some states later would tie voting rights with literacy. A drunken Union Army soldier literally writes the elder Macon Dead out of history when he goes to register with the Freedmen's Bureau (53). We should not ignore the irony of the event: an exercise meant to confirm his status as a freed man is the agent that obliterates his identity, and this excision acquires a stamp of permanence once it is written down.[11] *Song of Solomon* challenges this paradigm by locating the history of Macon and his parents not in the written text but in living memory, communal living memory.[12] In the words of Eleanor Branch, the novel "becomes an affirmation of tribal genealogy, a way to celebrate origins and connection, a way to immortalize those already dead" (53). The flight of Solomon and his wife Ryna's eternal sobbing in the woods find a repository in the community's folk song.

A number of critics have questioned the significance of Solomon's flight in the novel, suggesting that it entrenches a sexist notion of the dominance of the African American male.[13] But how far can these charges be sustained within the vernacular of the novel? To indict Solomon and, by extension, Milkman on the basis of their gender and the fate of Solomon's family left behind is to ignore the powerful cultural significance Morrison invests in capturing the flight itself. Milkman is not the only one to benefit from the unraveling of the song; Pilate's life journey acquires new meaning after Milkman returns with the full story about her ancestors.

The flight belongs to the grand scheme of the novel: to affirm the tradition from which the feat emanates. Song of Shalimar (Solomon) is the history of Solomon and his progeny, a history preserved and communicated to succeeding generations through a nonwritten medium in order to maintain its mythic value and its relevance to the community. It is also a demonstration of the community's active participation in the production and preservation of the black oral arts. The mock-heroic suicidal flight of Smith at the beginning of the novel contrasts with the heroic flight of Solomon, who regains his freedom by returning to Africa.[14] It is also through this song that families and communities spanning north to south of the country are able to trace their roots and consequently share a sense of connectedness. In this context, Gayl Jones's characterization of Solomon's flight as a "tall tale" misses Morrison's conceptualization of history and memory (174). Similarly, the flight should not be construed as a variant of the Western classical myth of Icarus and his father Daedalus, as some scholars have suggested.[15] Morrison herself debunks such thinking by stating categorically that she tries "to stay out of Western mythology" (Interview 461). Concerning her use of the flying African narrative, she says, "I'd always heard that black people could fly before they came to this country . . . and I decided not to treat [it] as some Western form of escape, and something more positive than escape. Suppose in a more dangerous element called air, learning how to trust, and knowing that much about one's self to the air, to surrender and control, both of those things. That's what that myth meant to me" (ibid. 463). Milkman's character portrait demonstrates the meaning that Morrison gleans from the story that African Americans often recount as actual incidents.[16] He steps out from the debilitating emotional environment that is his father's house and soars with the knowledge he acquires from his journey back to the South. There he unlearns everything he had learnt through association with his acquisitive father and his vengeful friend, Guitar. The apparent motion of flight that Milkman performs as he leaps toward Guitar firmly establishes it as a life-affirming (f)act (331). His heroism in the face of death and his self-sacrificing leap is a fitting alternative to Robert Smith's suicidal leap off the roof of Mercy Hospital.

The politics of written history, and its unreliability in representing the history of a marginalized people, forms the thesis of the novel. That is why, when finally the complete text of the song that has been appearing in broken forms in the novel, and which the reader now recognizes as the history of the Deads, is heard at the end of Milkman's journey, it resists the danger of being inert and unread in a written format. Milkman is compelled to commit it to memory, its sole legitimate agent of transmission.[17]

Furthermore, what is at issue is not fact or fantasy but the purpose and reason for its appropriation. As Milkman leaves the reluctant informant Susan Byrd, he contemplates what he has heard and what his dead father's ghost may have been trying to tell him at the cave: "Here he was walking around in the middle of the twentieth century trying to explain what a ghost had done. But why not? he thought. One fact was certain: Pilate did not have a navel. Since that was true, *anything could be,* and why not ghosts as well?" (294; emphasis added). The strength of Morrison's argument is that a novel that documents such known events and people as the Emmett Till murder and the rising national profile of Malcolm X is also capable of documenting the flight of an African slave back to Africa and the survival of the slave's children in a still racially stratified American society. Both the original leap by the ancestor Solomon and Milkman's fit Alejo Carpentier's definition of the marvelous as they demonstrate "an amplification of the scale and categories of reality, perceived with particular intensity by virtue of an exaltation of the spirit that leads it to a kind of extreme state" (86). *Song of Solomon* both recaptures the African American folktale tradition in writing and interrogates the hegemony of written linear history with its claims to factuality in accounting for the experience of African Americans. *Song of Solomon* evokes an alternative that eliminates the power of literacy over group identity by locating the latter squarely in the realm of myth preserved in communal living memory.

It is important to emphasize the value of oral narrative forms in *Song of Solomon*. Certainly, as Morrison's longest narrative to date, it spans a significant time frame and pursues a number of themes including black patriarchy, domestic abuse, and love. But as the title suggests, these themes are subsumed in the riddle of the song heard first at the beginning of the novel: Who is Sugarman? Where is home? Who is singing of flying Sugarman? Milkman's journey from Michigan to Pennsylvania helps solve the riddle, leading to the next question: why "Song"? Song indicates tribute, but more significantly, it draws attention to orality. In a wider sense the song is, to borrow Nora's term, a site of memory.

Morrison's lengthy narrative is a song (an epic?) performed in honor of the legend of the flying African ancestor. The tribute works on two levels: first, by relying on memory and folklore, Solomon's descendants circumvent the tyranny of the written word that has denied them equal access to the American national narrative and affirm their own history on their own terms. Solomon/Shalima/Sugarman, the African slave, did fly back to Africa. And as Macon tells Milkman about their ancestry, "If you ever doubt we from Africa, look at Pilate. She look just like Papa and he looked like all them pictures you ever see of Africans" (54). Second, the plurality of sources required to solve the riddle represents Morrison's firm recognition of history or group identity formation as communal. All the major informants—Macon Dead, Circe, Pilate, Susan Byrd—possess only partial claims to the full story. In typical oral narrative tradition, there is no individual authorship of the story; its continuity is dependent on the constant performance of the separate strands by the community as dictated by circumstance.

Contesting Memory, Interpreting Lettered Signs

In her seventh novel, *Paradise,* Morrison returns to the function of memory and oral tradition in defining black history and identity. Just as *Song of Solomon* portrays an African American family retrieving and preserving its genealogical tree through memory and active performance in the form of song, *Paradise* presents a community of African American migrants fashioning the history of their eventual settlement through memory and narrative. However, whereas the earlier novel focuses on the significance of the means by which the community preserves its identity, that is, memory and communally performed history, *Paradise* interrogates the neutrality of memory in fashioning the narrative of the community's past, especially when what is remembered serves to perpetuate a patriarchal order. In some ways, *Paradise* is a demonstration of Morrison's awareness of the complex nature of the African American historical experience, an experience that she is reluctant to represent in simple binarist or absolutist terms. Let me suggest that the novel is a logical progression on the kind of "aesthetic ideology" on which novels such as *Jazz* and *Song of Solomon* are based. That is, whereas these earlier novels seem to draw their "truth" from the extent to which the characters and authorial voices relate to black oral traditions, *Paradise* steps back to examine the uses of these oral agents of group identity. The novel presents a conflict between one group's "duty-memory" (Nora 292), that is, the group's resolve to remember their past in a certain way as a matter of duty, and another group's determination to experience that past in a liberating manner. This conflict between the older men and their children runs alongside the novel's focus on the lives of the women at the Convent in the present. Unlike the absence of a single version relating the founding of Haven and Ruby (even though the Morgans insist there is one), the reader is privy to the circumstances of the women's arrival at the Convent. From Mavis, who runs away from a threatening domestic space, to Gigi, who searches for (and later abandons) an elusive rendezvous with her jailed boyfriend, the narrator focuses on the process of the women's acceptance of each other under the tutelage of Consolata. It is almost as if their lives, accounted for in the present, repudiate the fetish the men have made of their communal memory.

Paradise is an imaginative discourse on the oral-written interface in African American culture. In earlier novels such as *Song of Solomon* and *Beloved,* memory is the interpretive sign. In *Paradise,* however, memory is interrogated as Morrison presents a slice of African American experience centered on the (ab)use of memory. This interrogation focuses on a community's response to oral and written history. Driving the narrative is a performer interested in representing the lore of her community's history, playing to the strengths of that community but also critical of certain aspects of that history. Morrison operates within the African American folkloric medium and invests the historical contents of her narratives with a mythic dimension.[18] The implication is clear: the resistance to empiricism and linearity, which defines mythic "truth," is coupled with the representation of African American reality. As Morrison explains elsewhere, black reality involves "the acceptance of the supernatural and a profound rootedness in the real world at the same time with neither taking precedence over the other" ("Rootedness" 342). The result of this coupling is a dynamic narrative vision capable of depicting black history without a betrayal of the deep oral roots of that history. *Paradise,* I would suggest, marks Morrison's clearest delineation of the uses of memory in representing the black experience in America, as an alternative to both the privileged medium of writing and the hegemonic power conferred on written and lineal history. The novel goes beyond celebrating the centrality of memory to black consciousness evidenced in *Beloved;* it delves into the very process of narrating what is remembered to reveal the myriad of interests that shape this narrative. At the end, the notion of a communal narrative generated by a common response to a past is seen as the catalyst for the various narrative performances that compete for acceptance in the text.

Set in mid-1976, amid the national trauma following the Vietnam War, *Paradise* presents the gradual death of Ruby, a community of fiercely proud black people, due to the refusal of its patriarchs to excise the cyst of an isolationism related to the circumstances of Ruby's founding. Around 1889, nine freed African American men, their families, and some strays from Mississippi and Louisiana band together in search of a settlement site in the Oklahoma Territory. They reach a town called Fairly, a settlement of fellow African Americans, and appeal to be allowed to join them. The request is rejected; the citizens of Fairly provide the migrants with victuals and ask them to move on. The migrants are quick to identify the cause of the rejection, later to be known as the Disallowing, as color. While the people of Fairly are lighter skinned, the migrants and their families are darker. Stung by this rejection, they travel without stopping until they find their own community, which they call Haven. Haven thrives for decades but later suffers from post–World War II depression. Descendants of the founders embark on another migration to a better land and Ruby, named for the woman who apparently died as a result of the hectic trek, is founded.

Ruby, an isolated town, "ninety miles from the nearest O for operator and ninety miles from the nearest badge" (13), is incidentally about seventeen miles from an old and obscure building housing a Catholic institution, Christ the King School for Native Girls, which the citizens of Ruby simply refer to as the Convent, despite the bold sign announcing its official name. Now in disrepair and no longer a schoolhouse, the Convent is inhabited and governed by the Mother Superior and her ward, Consolata (Connie), an orphan from South America, whom the nun had adopted. The Mother Superior dies at the beginning of the novel. Devastated by her death, Connie allows the Convent to sink further into ruins while turning it into a haven for women with various troubled histories. The persons and events in the Convent intersect to form the narrative of *Paradise.*

As leaders of the community, the men of Ruby maintain cohesion amid the growing dissent of the younger ones and the women by insisting on a particular narrative about the founding of the community and its predecessor, Haven. This narrative, incidentally, is far from written; it is a history kept alive in the memory of the older members, especially as remembered by the twins Deacon and Steward Morgan. Not only are the brothers the grandsons of Zechariah Morgan, known in Ruby's lore as Big Papa, the legendary leader of the first settlement at Haven, but they are also the most prosperous members of Ruby. "The twins," the narrator comments, "have powerful memories. Between them they remember the details of everything that ever happened—things they witnessed and things they have not. . . . And they have never forgotten the message or the specifics of any story, especially the *controlling* one told them by their grandfather" (13; emphasis added). Deacon is also described as possessing a "total memory" (107).

While the twins' recall capacity during oral recounting of Ruby's history follows the trajectory of remembering "things they witnessed and things they have not," the narrator nevertheless notes their insistence on a controlling narrative. Despite the disruptive or nonlineal dynamic of memory, especially in an oral performance medium, the Morgans' position points to a harnessing of what is remembered into what is literally a master narrative. The implication is that what is remembered and at the core of Ruby's "nationalism" is a narrative of a bruised male ego and a vengeful determination to reclaim it. There is also a class factor involved. The enormous economic power and social influence wielded by Steward and Deacon Morgan lead to a process of consciously choosing what they remember, and what they compel their fellow citizens to remember, about the principles and beliefs on which their community is founded.

In *Paradise,* the Oven symbolizes the strategy of harnessing what is otherwise a transgressive narrative medium for a coherent and "conservative" one. As Steward remembers the event, Big Papa prompted the men of Haven to build a cook oven. This facility not only served as a "community 'kitchen'" but was in fact a gesture of the men's pride "that none of their women had ever worked in a whiteman's kitchen or nursed a white child." Steward clearly favors this lofty reasoning for his grandfather's act even though Steward equally contemplates that "[m]aybe Zechariah never wanted to eat another stick-roasted rabbit, or cold buffalo meat" (99). The obvious appeal to the male ego that informs the making of the oven assumes an emblematic distinction when the twins and thirteen other families begin a fresh journey from Haven to Ruby, carrying the Oven with them. Once reassembled on the new site, it becomes the community's meeting place, and the men from the leading families confer on it the status of a totem.

However, a conflict between the younger sons of Ruby and their fathers arises over the correct missing words Big Papa had inscribed on the iron lids of the Oven. Were they "Be the Furrow of His Brow" or "Beware the Furrow of His Brow"? During its transport from Haven to Ruby, the letters of the first word in the meaning-laden statement had fallen off the Oven, leaving a gap that the two generations would contend to fill. The conflict over the missing word is at the center of a three-sided dialectic among controlled memory, the written word, and an unfettered "true memory." Although both sides understand the pronoun "His" to refer to God, the disagreement concerns the relationship of this powerful and fearsome God to His people, the black people of Ruby. The fathers vehemently declare that the statement is an order, hence the word is "Beware," for "God's justice is His alone." The younger generation, on the other hand, sees the message on the lid as a motto challenging the people to be "His instrument, His justice" (87).

The unspoken ideological argument is that the older generation of the Morgans, who insist on retaining the isolationist and patriarchal order instituted by the original freed men, desire to use the Oven as an instrument of social cohesion. The power and reverence to God that they argue the words on the lid represent are a ruse for the unchallenged authority they demand. The interpretation by Harper Jury, the son of one of the founders of Haven, reflects this unspoken bias: "It says, 'Beware.' Not 'Be.' Beware means 'Look out. The power is mine. Get used to it'" (87). Deacon Morgan says categorically, "Nobody, I mean nobody, is going to change the Oven or call it something strange. Nobody is going to mess with a thing our grandfathers built" (85). His brother Steward also wonders what the founders "would think of those puppies who wanted to alter words of beaten iron" (99). For the older men, the Oven is a solidification of a remembered past.

There is an irony in the disagreement that divides Ruby in two, and it does not lie in the elliptical life of the words on the Oven. The irony is that the critically ambiguous words of the patriarch, which have become "worn letters" (6) on the Oven, betray one primary virtue of writing—permanence, an ability to "preserve the word from vanishing" (Biakolo 88). In contrast to Walter Ong's assertion that the written word has the "potential of being lifted and placed on different places, or being resurrected" (*Interfaces of the Word* 156), the written words on the lid of the Oven disappear, creating a rift among Ruby's inhabitants. The irony deepens when, in order to prove their own version of the missing word, the twins and the other men call on Esther, the eighty-year-old sole surviving member of the Haven settlers, to tell the community what she remembers about the word on the Oven. The young people ridicule what they call Esther's "finger memory," peeved "at the notion of remembering invisible words you couldn't even read by tracing letters you couldn't pronounce":[19]

"Did you see them?" asked the sons.
"Better than that!" shouted the fathers. "She felt them, touched them, and put her fingers on them!"
"If she was blind, Sir, we could believe her. That'd be like braille. But some five-year-old kid who couldn't read her own tombstone if she climbed out of her grave and stood in front of it?" (83)

In the heated debate, the fathers invoke the authority of a living witness to authenticate their interpretation of a text that not even the testimony of a witness can validate. Like the elder Macon Dead in *Song of Solomon*, who is betrayed by the power of literacy, Esther's memory and belief in the infallibility of the written word is vitiated by her inability to read. Whatever she thinks she remembers, contrary to the thinking of the men who depend on her testimony, cannot be so easily traced on the impersonal contours of the engraved words[20]—a point the sons emphasize.

The misalignment between what is remembered, traced, and felt on the fingers marks a paradigm shift that *Paradise* problematizes. The missing letters constitute a nebulous space in which Morrison interrogates the permanence or durability of the written word or documented history. Yet she points to the potential of oral histories, even when recounted by someone who "felt them, touched them, put her fingers on them," to be channeled toward a political end. In *Song of Solomon*, there is no obvious special interest within the black community in preserving the story of Shalimar in a particular way (even though the village belle, Sweet, would sarcastically ask Milkman, concerning his great-grandfather's flight, "who'd he leave behind?" [328]). What is embedded in the communal consciousness in the earlier novel is both the affirmation of the story of the ancestor and the presence of dissenting or disinterested voices, like Susan Byrd's and Sweet's, who are at liberty to question the usefulness of the Shalimar narrative. In *Paradise,* the men are determined to submerge the compositeness of communal memory[21]—the missing letters on the iron lid of the Oven—in favor of an orchestrated narrative that kills the creative force of the community represented by the imperative verb, "Be."

The leading men of Ruby nurture and retain memory of their humiliation by fellow black men, albeit of a lighter complexion; not content to found a place of their own, they build one that resists any dissent and any form of freedom not made in their own image. In this way, the novel raises a pertinent issue on the limits of the use of the memories of the past. Is what is remembered to be a furrow, an impediment to the creative conscious of the present, or a catalytic agent capable of transforming the present? The Methodist priest Richard Misner, a non-native and the rallying point for the younger people, perceives the trouble with Ruby's sense of its past:

> Over and over and with the least provocation, they [Ruby citizens] pulled from their stock of stories tales about the old folks, their grands and greatgrands; their fathers and mothers. Dangerous confrontations, clever maneuvers. Testimonies to endurance, wit, skill and strength. Tales of luck and outrage. But why were there no stories to tell of themselves? About their own lives they shut up. Had nothing to say, pass on. As though past heroism was enough of a future to live by. As though, rather than children, they wanted duplicates. (161)

It is not that the older men do not have stories of themselves to tell; they have fought as American soldiers in foreign lands, and their courageous decision to move away from Haven to a new land could well translate to stories of heroism. The reason for their silence about themselves is that the Morgans and the other men who share their vision of a community recognize the power of the oral tradition, the political and religious power that a mythic narrative of the past has for coercing conformity.

Yet *Paradise* is far from presenting a single narrative about Ruby. Events—past and present—constitute keenly agonistic spaces for narrative performance by the key characters. Three main levels of narration operate in the novel: the twins' recollections provide one layer of account; the voices of Patricia Best, Dovey and Soane Morgan (the two sisters who are married to the twins), Consolata, and Lone DuPres make up varying degrees of a counternarrative to that of the twins; and, finally, an authorial voice acts as the reader's interpreter. Among the three perspectives, the authorial voice constantly redirects the reader to composite narratives. This practice enables the reader to witness the partial or even dubious manipulation of a received tradition by the performing characters. As readers we are in the presence of story-making, but like the characters in the novel we are denied the privilege of omniscience. Nobody knows. Thus, the narrative structure effectively exposes the impracticability of the kind of narrative that the Morgans and the men want to foist on Ruby.

Different narrative moods distinguish the men's narrative from the women's. The Morgan twins' recollections are evoked with a masculine sense of infallibility; they have no reason to doubt the stories their father, Rector, handed down to them. Besides, some of their claims of authority rest on their personal recollection of events. More significantly, the brothers promote their personal memory as synonymous with the community's. A rhetorical forcefulness characterizes such an enormous leap from the private to the public. One striking example of the twins' controlling performance occurs at the same venue where Esther's "finger memory" is ridiculed. Irked by the young people's boldness in questioning their elders' reverence of the Oven, Deacon responds with characteristic specificity, calling on his colleagues to bear witness:

> *They* [the founding fathers] dug the clay—not you. They carried the hod— not you. . . . They mixed the mortar—not a one of you. They made good strong brick for that oven when their own shelter was sticks and sod. You understand what I'm telling you? And *we* respected what they had gone through to do it. Nothing was handled more gently than the bricks those men—men, hear me? not slaves, ex or otherwise—the bricks those men made. Tell them, Sargeant, how delicate was the separation, how careful we were, how we wrapped them, each and every one. Tell them, Fleet. You, Seawright, you, Harper, you tell him if I'm lying. *Me and my brother lifted that iron. The two of us.* (85–86; emphasis added)

While Deacon recounts what is evidently a communal lore, the institution of the Oven, we observe a gradual shift from representing the efforts of the patriarchs ("they"), to courting the solidarity of his fellow men ("we"), and finally to resting the weight of his entire speech on the action of him and his brother Steward. Deacon does not make a distinction between received tradition and his own personal narrative; for example, he was not at the oven-making ceremony to know the specifics of the construction—digging the clay, carrying the hod, and so forth. But the reference is necessary in order to reinforce the events in which he is a participant and, now, the narrator.[22] This performance strategy is not lost on Royal Beauchamp (Roy), one of the leading speakers for the youths, who retorts on charges that his peers want to kill the Oven's value in this way: "It's our history too, sir. Not just yours" (86). Deacon's act is a powerful appropriation of communal narrative that relies on realigning the key parts of that repertoire to serve the speaker's purpose.

The founding of Haven is remembered and narrated in mythic proportions. This is not surprising; the narration is from the subject position of Steward, who "remembered every detail of the story his father and grandfather told" (95). After the Disallowing, and in righteous anger, Big Papa, who is lame, urges the people on an uninterrupted trek. On the third night, while the other trekkers are resting, Zechariah takes his only son, Rector, far into the woods to pray. In a scene reminiscent of Christ's intense emotional torment in the Garden of Gethsemane,[23] Zechariah remains on his knees, "hum[ming] the sweetest, saddest sounds" in prayer (96), while Rector, like Christ's disciples, cannot keep up and apparently falls asleep. Big Papa's reported opening words of prayer are striking: "My Father, Zechariah here." It echoes the intimacy with God that such biblical figures as Abraham, Moses, Samuel, and Christ experienced. In Gethsemane, angels minister to Christ to strengthen him for the journey to the cross. As for Big Papa and Rector, they hear thundering footsteps and then, "A small man, seemlike, too small for the sound of his steps," wearing a "glistening white" shirt appears (97). Zechariah's bad foot is miraculously restored, and from that point the small man, seen by only Zechariah, leads the families for twenty-nine days until he brings them to the appointed place, preceded by a supernatural sign. Like the ancient Israelites who were led through the desert by fire in the night and cloud by day, Zechariah follows behind the loud footsteps of the unidentified man.

The Disallowing is Ruby's unifying narrative: "Afterwards the people were no longer nine families and some more. They became a tight band of wayfarers bound by the enormity of what had happened to them" (189). Further on, the narrator remarks, "Everything anybody wanted to know about the citizens of Haven or Ruby lay in the ramifications of that one rebuff out of many." The unspoken rule not to have any dealings with white people or with blacks with lighter skin emerges from this encounter: "Their horror of whites was convulsive but abstract. They saved the clarity of their hatred for the men who had insulted them in ways too confounding for language: first by excluding them, then by offering them staples to exist in that very exclusion" (189).[24] The deep-seated hatred for persons of mixed race, however, creates a rupture in an otherwise morally persuasive narrative, in that the hatred accounts for the efforts by the leading families to tactfully erase some details of the original persons who began the journey to Haven and, later, to Ruby.

The men of Ruby nurture and retain the memory of their humiliation. They give the incident a name of epic dimensions—the Disallowing—which they use as an instrument for silencing or ostracizing members of the community who are not as dark as members of the founding families. Patricia Best, the counternarrative performer in the novel, aptly calls the core families "8-R. An abbreviation for eight-rock, a deep deep level in the coal mines" (193). Memories of images of their ideal black women also cast a long shadow over their standards of what is acceptable conduct for women. This shadow is the instigator for the mid-July 1976 attack on the women living in the Convent. The five women there not only live an uncensored life but also are free of male control: "The whole house [the Convent] felt permeated with a blessed malelessness, like a protected domain, free of hunters but exciting too" (177). The xenophobic attitude of the men and their repulsion at the women in the Convent are projected as justified because of the twins' biased rendering of a communal narrative.

Set against the endorsed oral and remembered history of Haven and Ruby is a counter (documented) text being assembled by Patricia Best, a schoolteacher and daughter of Roger Best, one of the nine cofounders of Ruby. The community treats father and daughter, as well as Patricia's daughter, Billie Delia, as outsiders and morally tainted persons because Roger broke the unspoken code by "marrying a wife with no last name, a wife without people, a wife of sunlight skin, a wife of racial tampering" (197). From her forced position as an outsider among her own people, and given her limited influence as a woman in Ruby's patriarchal society, Patricia initiates an unraveling of the common ancestral narrative as peddled by the powerful male authority in Ruby. Rather than rely on the remembered accounts—known in detail only by the men and performed by the children in place of the nativity story—Patricia chooses to assemble a counternarrative based on written evidence:

> The town's official story, elaborated from pulpits, in Sunday school classes and ceremonial speeches, had a sturdy public life. Any footnotes, crevices or questions to be put took keen imagination and the persistence of a mind uncomfortable with oral histories. Pat had wanted proof in

documents where possible to match the stories, and where proof was not
available she interpreted—freely but, she thought, insightfully because
she alone had the required emotional distance. She alone could figure out
why a line was drawn through Ethan Blackhorse's name in the Blackhorse
Bible and what the heavy ink blot hid next to Zechariah's name in the
Morgan Bible. (188)

The written records sought by Patricia present another instance of the
novel's parodying of the written text. As the instrument of state power, the
written word is the preferred medium for the preservation or execution
of authority in the public domain. It is retrievable, "citable," and carefully
composed with an eye to its relevance to and applicability in the future.

Patricia's historiographical credo, on the other hand, depends on the
minute acts of intimacy conferred upon the otherwise impersonal written
word. Far from the public space where the patriarchal narrative holds sway,
the personal names on books—those blotted or crossed out, and the individual histories of their families that Patricia's young students produce—are
the narrative strands that she uses to question and undermine the master
narrative. Moreover, her historiography provides a space for "de-inking"
the blotted names for a more expansive and embracing narrative of the
founding of Haven and Ruby, a narrative in which the lives and contributions of other citizens excluded from the "official story" are included.[25]
Of those disadvantaged persons, the most visible (by their invisibility) are
the women, known by their first names and by their affiliation through
marriage to the 8-rock families. Patricia, contemplating the fate of her
mother, Delia, and other women who had died, wonders: "Who were these
women who, like her mother, had only one name? Celeste, Olive, Sorrow,
Ivlin, Pansy. Who were these women with generalized last names? Brown,
Smith, Rivers, Stone, Jones. Women whose identity rested on the men they
married—if marriage applied: a Morgan, a Flood, a Blackhorse, a Poole, a
Fleetwood" (187–88). It is significant that in representing the history of her
own family in the project, the third-person point of view disappears, giving
way to Patricia's first-person journal entry as she addresses her parents
(196–202). This is the only place in the novel where first-person narration
ensues, highlighting Patricia's manipulation of the individualistic act of
writing in drawing meaning out of the experiences of her parents.

Patricia's genealogical tree therefore restores the several branches
pruned to feed a sexist vision. For example, the blotted name beside Zechariah's in the Morgan family Bible belongs to Tea, Zechariah's twin brother,
and Zechariah's name at birth was Coffee (302). Tea's name erasure is an

external act in the process of obliterating his memory as the one who "quite reasonably" complies with the command of two drunk and gun-toting white men to dance. Zechariah had refused and was shot in the foot for his disobedience.[26] Ashamed of his twin brother's ready compliance, Zechariah invited two other men and together they gathered other families for the trek that led them to Haven, leaving Tea behind. Tea's name is blotted out because his action of obliging the white men with a dance is antithetical to the 8-rock's narrative that they have never bowed to any white person. Nor have their wives. Moreover, it enhances the process of mythologizing Zechariah as a combined Moses and Christ figure. Similarly, Patricia's performance reveals the lie in the men's aversion to whiteness; they had no problems in using Delia's light complexion to gain access to places from which they otherwise would have been barred (200).

The unraveling of such repressed histories as the identity of Zechariah's twin brother does not compare with the greater significance that the resurrection of the women's names has for the understanding of the major sources of conflict in the novel. Women in *Paradise* are the wise silent observers of the men and their puny emotional outbursts. The women see through the hypocrisy and shallowness of the men's thinking, thereby projecting visions of another world, another black world, where the benefits of emancipation and the civil rights movement have not been stillborn or thwarted by the foolishness, the acrid hatred, and meanness of their men. While the male founders of Ruby fight doggedly to protect their narcissistic sentiments about their community, and in the process suppress dynamic social forces, the women are perceptive enough to discern the conflicts and dismiss them as mere egotistical sallies.

Consider Dovey, Steward's wife. Alone and thinking about the meeting of the older men and their children over the original words on the iron lids of the Oven, she ponders with Christian philosophical flair: "'Beware the Furrow of His Brow?' 'Be the Furrow of His Brow?' Her own opinion was that 'Furrow of His Brow' alone was enough for any age or generation. Specifying it, particularizing it, nailing its meaning down, was futile. The only nailing needing to be done had already taken place. On the Cross" (93). Dovey's meditation articulates the novel's larger argument. At first appearing passive, her words are remarkably postmodernist and radical in their resistance to specificity. They are calls for each generation to interpret its past in the manner relevant to it, rather than be slaves to the past. Besides, she expounds on the dynamic nature of narratives, the idea that context, audience, and individual temperament of the performer determine the contents of the narrative.

Except for advocating Dovey's opinion, there is no clear indication about the veracity of the source of the conflict. In Patricia's version, the words are a "conundrum" deliberately wrought by Zechariah with utmost linguistic ambiguity:

> "Beware the Furrow of His Brow," in which the "You" (understood), vocative case, was not a command to the believers but a threat to those who had disallowed them. It must have taken him months to think up those words—just so—to have multiple meanings: to appear stern, urging obedience to God, but slyly not identifying the understood proper noun or specifying what the Furrow might cause to happen or to whom. So the teenagers Misner organized who wanted to change it to "Be the Furrow of His Brow" were more insightful than they knew. (195)

Impressive as Patricia's semantic analysis is, the novel does not allow the reader to surrender to any single perspective for meaning. In the case of the vexatious words, earlier on in the novel, one of the unidentified men who attack the Convent expresses doubts about the source of the words attributed to Zechariah Morgan: "It is still not clear where the words came from. Something he heard, invented, or something whispered to him while he slept curled over his tools in a wagon bed. His name was Morgan and who knew if he invented or stole the half-dozen or so words he forged" (7). It is clear that the entire community—not even among the men who accompany the twins to the assault on the Convent women—does not completely share whatever greatness Zechariah's children and grandchildren attribute to him.

In Ruby, the past remembered by a select few has degenerated into a cold, oppressive ideology of intolerance. Delia Best, Patricia's mother, dies in childbirth because her 8-rock neighbors would rather watch her bleed to death than invite a white doctor into the community to save her. Worse still, her death would mean the elimination of what they consider a blot on Ruby—a light complexion. Concealed within the genealogies of many of the leading families are cases of incest committed in order to avoid marrying into a non-8-rock bloodline (196). Following the attack on the women at the Convent, and the consequent communal shock and embarrassment at the incident, the closed world of Ruby falls apart. The young people represent this anomie by attacking the words on the Oven: "No longer were they calling themselves Be the Furrow of His Brow. The graffiti on the hood of the Oven now was 'We are the Furrow of His Brow'" (298). It is a tragic epitaph for a grand nationalist design, which in its attempt to express the dignity of a community exchanges that vision for a narrow and constricted one.

It is perhaps in Lone DuPres that Morrison imbues the most penetrating understanding of the hollowness of the men's thinking. She is one of Ruby's oldest citizens, the only midwife and a reputed seer who actually "practices." Like Patricia, Lone is part of the community and yet lives as an outsider who in her ruminations perceives the rapid changes occurring in Ruby. Fairy DuPres, a teenage member of the original pilgrims, had rescued Lone as a little child. Fairy had found her sitting alone by the doorpost of a hut, half-starved with her mother dead and lying in the hut. Against the urging of the men who felt they did not have enough food to feed another hungry mouth, Fairy refused to abandon the baby and named her Lone because of the circumstance of her rescue.

Although it appears that Lone's interventions at critical situations in the novel are merely coincidental, there is a strong suggestion that she is like the biblical lone "voice of one crying in the wilderness."[27] She appears to be the only person in Ruby who understands the troubled lives of the women who eventually wander into the Convent. She alone understands the haven the women find there. On the night of the nine men's predawn attack on the Convent, Lone stumbles into their conspiracy and rushes to tell the women at the Convent about the plot. Unfortunately, they do not believe her, and, desperately, she drives back to wake up her fellow villagers to dissuade the men from carrying out their plan. As she drives from the Convent back to Ruby in her worn single-headlight Oldsmobile, she thinks about the significance of the road:

> it was women who walked this road. Only women. Never men. For more
> than twenty years Lone had watched them. Back and forth, back and forth:
> crying women, staring women, scowling, lip-biting women or women just
> plain lost ... women dragged their sorrow up and down the road between
> Ruby and the Convent. They were the only pedestrians. . . . But the men
> never walked the road; they drove it, although sometimes their destina-
> tion was the same as the women's. (270)

It is this accurate understanding of the fate of the women in her male-dominated society that compels her to try, though unsuccessfully, to stop the men.

More significantly, Lone is the only character who divines the real reason behind the men's attack. At their nocturnal meeting, the men allege that the Convent women are polluting the moral atmosphere of Ruby by their apparent amorous or amoral lifestyle. It does not matter that, unbeknownst to all the men but Steward, Deacon Morgan had in the past had a passionate affair with Consolata. The men accuse the women of infanticide, mass murders, and the seduction of Ruby's young ones. Lone reverses this grievous narrative by helping the reader make connections with incidents narrated earlier that expose the falsehood of the men's allegations. That the nine men choose to act from sheer ignorance and pigheadedness is one of the high points of this novel; what is frightening is the dangerously sexist underpinning of this misconception. The men consider their impending aggression against the women as a moral necessity ("these here sluts out there by themselves never step foot in Church and I bet you a dollar to a fat nickel that they ain't thinking about one either. . . . They meddle. Drawing folks out there like flies to shit and everybody who goes near them is maimed somehow and the mess is seeping back into *our* homes, *our* families" [276]). Lone rightly understands that the men's actual grudge is that the Convent is a "house full of women. Not women locked safely away from men; but worse, women who chose themselves for company" (276).

As Lone eavesdrops on the men's secret meeting, she comments on the narrative the men have chosen to believe to justify their invasion: "Here, when the men spoke of a ruination that was upon them—how Ruby was changing in intolerable ways—they did not think to fix it by extending a hand in fellowship or love. They mapped defense instead and honed evidence for its need, till each piece fit an already polished groove" (275). Lone's observation touches on the central argument of the novel. The men refuse to see the unwinding threads of Ruby's society and fixate instead on the sentimental value of a controlled memory of their past. They are determined, as they rampage the Convent, "[t]hat nothing inside or out rots the one all-black town worth the pain" (5). In their misguided representation of themselves as defenders of their society's ideals, the novel portrays them as dangerous zealots who cripple the promise of an otherwise lofty enterprise.

Unlike most of Morrison's previous novels, in which she focuses on individuals and their relationship to the community, *Paradise* is a narrative on Ruby. The conflicts in the novel relate to the charting of Ruby's destiny based on how the people perceive or are led to perceive their past and its relationship to their well-being. The novel pits the "total" domineering memory of the Morgans against the cold and guided written document of Patricia Best. However, the presence of Lone DuPres suggests that Morrison refrains from offering a straight-laced binary depiction of this African

American society. Lone, the rejected midwife, feared because of her spiritual powers, is the one character who "know[s] something more profound than Morgan memory or Pat Best's history book. She knew what neither memory nor history can say or record: the 'trick' of life and its 'reason'" (272).

Paradise is perhaps Morrison's clearest articulation of the fallacy in attributing any form of narrative—oral or written—to either the oppressed or the oppressor. What she suggests is that these positions (subject and form) are not permanent. Between the blacks in Fairly who turn away their darker-skinned freed men and women, and the men of Haven who try to erase the presence of the Bests because of their color, there is no difference. What unites them is power. The oppressive role oral narrative plays in *Paradise* confirms Kerwin Lee Klein's argument in his critique of Lyotard's conceptualization of the terms "master narrative" and "local stories." According to Klein, "No special way of telling can guarantee that today's local narrative will not become tomorrow's narrative master. Virtually overnight, the chanting of subaltern protest may modulate into the crack of the historical whip" (297).

The men's fossilization of Ruby's history through their selective memory recall is rejected because it delegitimizes parallel narratives in the rapidly changing fortunes of Ruby. Significant as orality is in the African American aesthetic, *Paradise* rejects this particular performance by the men by revealing how dangerously malleable the spoken text can be. After the attack on the women, several versions—or "editions," as Patricia Best calls them—of what happened emerge. Again, it is Lone who is "unhinged by the way the story was being retold; how people were changing it to make themselves look good." She sees how relatives of the men involved, with their varying exculpatory versions, "supported them [the versions], enhancing, recasting, inventing misinformation" (297). This is one place where Morrison, with an unflinching gaze, shows us the making of an oral narrative and the challenges it poses to a Grand Story. No one in Ruby is able to explain the mysterious disappearance of the Convent women, both the murdered and the survivors; and Morrison does not assist the reader, either.

Like the oral tale whose first teller or "author" can hardly be identified, the truth about the fate of the women will never be verified. The narrator consciously leaves the women's disappearance and their later "manifestations" on the mythic plane. Lone refers to the various versions of the Convent attack as "altered truth," but reading the uses the men have made of the event's mystery solidifies the novel's argument about the capacity of the spoken word to authenticate power. Conversely, the incomplete endorsement of the alternative represented by Patricia Best's genealogical tree project is based on its similar inability to account for the whole truth. Conscientious as she is in accounting for every person in Ruby, she cannot avoid the trappings of individuality that writing fosters, as she adopts a more intimate perspective in representing the lives of her parents. No wonder that, in a strange twist of events, Patricia throws the entire project into a fire, thus extinguishing the existence of her written countertext. Morrison directs her artistic vision to the unknown quantity in African American experience, the "trick" of life that defies any unitary narrative.

Dissonant Notes and Narrative Authority

Paradise suggests that Morrison resists a compartmentalization of both her artistic and ideological positions. The "trick of life" to which the seer Lone refers encapsulates the philosophy that guides the novelist's works. Rather than the pursuit of simple themes with tidy endings and solutions, Morrison situates her novels in spaces of surprise. The surprise element is an acknowledgment of the unpredictability that characterizes social interactions and events at large. There is a twofold manifestation of this principle in *Jazz*. The first is the novel as a discourse on interpersonal relationships, and the other is the novel as a discourse on narrative voice. In both areas, Morrison focuses on "the 'trick' of life and its 'reason'" as a way of displacing her audience since life's major trace is this uncertainty.

My discussion of *Song of Solomon* and *Paradise* highlights Morrison's close attachment to history as the defining agent of African American life. The African American worldview she presents is informed by the peculiar history she explores in her novel. *Jazz* focuses on the African American Great Migration narrative. While Violet, the major female character, and the other women play a crucial role in defining the nature and significance of relationships in the novel, Morrison portrays them along the unwinding thread of 1920s African American history and the representation of that history by the artist (the narrator). As demonstrated in *Paradise*, the success of the black community rests on its use of history.

In *Jazz*, there is a continued gaze on African American history; but it is a shifting or playful gaze that suggests Morrison's subtle resistance to a simplification of that history. In her essay "Following the Traces of Female Desire in Toni Morrison's *Jazz*," Elizabeth Cannon argues that the novel is "theorizing the nature of desire, particularly African-American female desire, and its effect on narrative" (235). Perhaps it is more correct to assert that the novel theorizes the nature of narrative, written narrative to be precise. The narrative of the 1920s Great Migration from the South is an important one in the life and history of African Americans. The narrative posture adopted by Morrison in this novel captures one of the "tricky" aspects of this epoch. Morrison has noted that one of the attributes of African American art is "the ability to be both print and oral literature" ("Rootedness" 341). This may be regarded as a reiteration of W. E. B. DuBois's notion of "double-consciousness" (8), but in the novel, it plays out as the celebratory voice of an artist combining the improvisational dynamic of an oral performance with the controlled exercise of a written medium.

The narrator in *Jazz* is united with an imagined immediate audience. It is not an audience of strangers; the narrator assumes the audience to be composed of persons familiar to her, readers to whom she can relate. The narrative "I" in the novel erupts with casual unpredictability. Here the "I" is conversational, as in the novel's opening statement, "I know that woman," and, throughout, the narrator addresses an implied listening/observing/reading audience. By positioning the narrator in this way, Morrison creates a written voice and a space akin to the artistic and social exchange between the artist and audience in an oral performance context.

The communality of the performance space is further demonstrated by the multiple narrative voices. At various points in the novel, each character speaks in first person. It is as if the characters are making a direct appeal to the audience, asking to be understood, asking for a space to *speak* and not be spoken about by a self-conscious narrator. For example, as the narrator who claims to know Joe Trace "too well" (119) proffers her explanation for the middle-aged man's short-lived romance with teenage Dorcas, which ends with Joe killing the woman, the narrator concludes: "No wonder it ended the way it did." Then she continues, "But it didn't have to, and if he had stopped trailing that little fast thing all over town long enough to tell Stuck or Gistan or some neighbor who might be interested, who knows how it would go?" (121). Joe's "defense" in his own voice begins at this point: "It is not a thing you tell another man," he says, inviting the reader to be his confessor. In other words, he does not leave the reader wondering about the outcome or about his real motivation for doing what he has done, as the narrator does. This is a narrative framing that reveals the compositeness of truth. A similar compositeness of narrative perspective is attained in the sections where Violet speaks (89–101). Dorcas, in her death throes, is able to see the final moments of her life and narrate it in her own voice as well (189–93).

The interaction between the narrator and the (other) characters further exemplifies the communal narrative performance.[28] The constant shifts from an omniscient point of view to a first-person singular where the narrator directly breaks into the consciousness of the characters recall a similar device in oral performance. A raconteur not only tells a tale; sometimes s/he also questions the action of the characters. In dramatic scenarios, it is possible for the narrator to enter into dialogue with the characters or interweave the ongoing story with his or her own "personal" narrative. Such an interaction is prevalent in *Jazz*. One instance of interlocking narrative occurs where the narrator has finished recounting how Dorcas was spurned at a party by some "brothers" because of her looks. The incident is narrated to explain why she entertained Joe's courting, and it is presented in third person:

> So by the time Joe Trace whispered to her through the crack of a closing door her life had become almost unbearable. Almost. The flesh, heavily despised by the brothers, held secret the love appetite soaring inside it. *I've seen swollen fish, serenely blind, floating in the sky. Without eyes, but somehow directed, these airships swim below cloud foam and nobody can be turned away from the sight of them because it's like watching a private dream.* That was what her hunger was like: mesmerizing, directed, floating like a public secret just under the cloud cover. (67; emphasis added)

The "I" interjection at this point in the narrative creates a dual viewpoint by suggesting that the "I" is a mediator between the reader and a third-person omniscient narrator. In addition, even though the highlighted portion is intrusive, it is a useful amplification of the emotional condition of Dorcas, as effective as a Homeric simile. Sometimes, though, the interruptions are no more than unsolicited opinions and quips from a busybody gossip. Consider, for example, the following narration:

> From Malvonne [Violet] learned [Dorcas's] address and whose child she was. From the legally licensed beauticians she found out what kind of lip rouge the girl wore; the marcelling iron they used on her (though I suspect that girl didn't need to straighten her hair); the band the girl liked best (Slim Bates' Ebony Keys which is pretty good except for his vocalist who must be his woman since why else would he let her insult his band). (5)

A narrator who surreptitiously watches the unfolding drama of the characters' lives provides the parenthetical remarks for the benefit of the reader. They are not as relevant to the characters' psychological development as they are indicative of a folksy narrator, a member of the community, idle perhaps, who trades on minding other people's business: "I always believed that girl [Dorcas] was a pack of lies. I could tell by her walk her under-clothes were beyond her years, even if her dress wasn't" (72).

The question may be asked, how can a narrator like the one in *Jazz* execute the "serious" task of revisiting a people's experience with credi-bility? The answer lies in, again, grasping Morrison's notion of narratives in relation to a people's understanding of themselves. Morrison refuses to set an unbending philosophical framework for her use or representation of African American life; instead, she reflects on each movement in black experience with a measure of "specificity."[29] The result is that her repre-sentation of African American life through the experiences of characters in her novels is a complex one, unpossessed of simple notions. The narra-tor embodies the complexity. In addition to delineating African American characters who embody aspects of black experience in the United States, *Jazz* "performs" the narrative of a narrator whose very personality *is* the problem with our understanding of the myriad experiences that constitute African American culture and tradition.

There is a remarkable superficiality to the narrator's character judg-ments. She describes herself as "curious, inventive and well-informed" (137), and about Joe Trace she says, "I know him so well" (119). Seeing the complicated relationship joining the characters—from Wild to Golden Gray to Dorcas to Joe to Felice to Violet—from the narrator's presumptuous eyes evokes a picture of angst, of abject despair without hope. The emotionally tortuous relationship between Joe and Violet, following Joe's murder of Dorcas and Violet's attack on the dead woman, surprisingly heals "under a sweetheart weather" (195). Surprising, because as the narrator concedes in the final segment of the novel, which could be described as a narratological self-critique, "I was sure one would kill the other . . . I was so sure" (220).

The same mistaken assumption is identifiable in the parallel-running story of Golden Gray. The narrator interprets every gesture the young man makes from the moment he decides to help the half-dead naked woman to his eventual encounter with Henry, "Hunters Hunter," with hardly con-cealed spite and bitterness. She calls the biracial character a "hypocrite" (154) and a "vain and hincty pinch-nose" who "insult[s] . . . his race" (143) through his uppity conduct. The narrator's opinion is stock and predictable and shows no effort to understand the situation from Golden Gray's posi-tion. Unbeknownst to him, while growing up far away from the plantation where his mother had been forced into exile, Golden Gray is a product of a forbidden sexual relationship between Vera Louise, daughter of a white plantation owner, and Henry, a black field hand. Devastated by the discovery that his father is a black laborer, Golden Gray is urged by True Belle, his mother's servant and Violet's grandmother, to go back and find his father, for as she says, "It don't matter if you do find him or not; it's the going that counts" (159). This is the crux of the story, the anxiety of racial reconciliation that cannot be accomplished by the cynical attitude of the narrator to the inquirer.

From his genteel and pampered world, Golden Gray descends to the foggy and muddy precipice of his origins and gets drenched in the pain and humiliation of the enterprise. Golden Gray is the presence in African American, indeed, American history that cannot be erased or brushed aside by the caustic observations of the self-righteous narrator of *Jazz*. The narrator expresses her sentiments about him based on the superficial polarities of white and black. Golden Gray, for instance, learns that his revealed identity changes his prior shallow idea of blackness: "He had always thought there was only one kind—True Belle's kind. Black and nothing. Like Henry LesTroy . . . But there was another kind—like himself" (149). Similarly, when father and son finally meet, Hunters Hunter exhibits neither bitterness nor joy at the encounter. He is more concerned about the daily struggles of living than analyzing color and accepting the young man simply on that basis. He tells Golden Gray, with the impatience of a father, "Be what you want—White or black. Choose. But if you choose black, you got to act black, meaning draw your manhood up—quicklike, and don't bring me no whiteboy sass" (173). In other words, blackness, or for that matter, whiteness, goes beyond appearance or even blood; one "acquires" identity through what one makes of one's peculiar history.

For Golden Gray, the search for roots is not without anxiety. Contrary to the impression created by the narrator that he is a brat more concerned about his clothing than about helping Wild, his words reflect the trauma he faces as he waits for the return of Hunters Hunter. He likens his previous ignorance of who his father is to a missing arm and wonders, "When I find it, will it wave to me? Gesture, beckon to me to come along? Or will it even know who or what I am?" (159). There are no easy answers to these questions, as the encounter between the two men reveals. However, this is a critical search that must be undertaken because, as Golden Gray puts it concerning the lost arm, he must "locate it so the severed part can remember the snatch, the slice of its disfigurement" (159). We must thank the direct speech of the character for offering a rounded perspective on the conflict. By implication, Morrison challenges the reader to interrogate the received information of the narrator and not take the narrator's point of view as necessarily reliable or truthful.[30]

Since the publication of the novel, there has been a heated debate about the connection of its title with jazz.[31] It is not surprising that arguments have arisen, considering that the novel is set in the 1920s, a period that, in addition to being the era of the Great Migration northward, was also the golden age of jazz; thus the contemporaneous emergence of both phenomena makes the comparison of the novel with that musical form very attractive. Besides, the informal and extemporaneous remarks of the narrator may be compared to the improvisational nature of jazz. Yet to take the analysis only to the point where these similarities exist is to miss a more fundamental aesthetic paradigm at play in the novel. The last segment of the novel, in which the narrator is unmasked,[32] is the ultimate demonstration of Morrison's "tricks."[33] Just as the presumptions of the narrator on the responses of the characters and their outcome end up being unfounded, the novel calls into question some aspects of African American history that have become received wisdom: more specifically, the wisdom peddled by the populist ideologues whom the narrator in *Jazz* represents.

The open-endedness of Morrison's narratives and, by extension, her construction of (black) experience are based on the riddle idiom. As Richard Bauman rightly states, "Riddles and related enigmatic genres turn, characteristically, on ambiguity and multiplicity of meaning" ("Three Guesses" 62). This is true of Morrison's novels. In *Jazz*, it is in the form of representing the complexity of narrativity by looking at the unpredictability of the narrative temperament.

The common signifier in the three novels examined is Morrison's investment in exploring the dimensions of the black narrative. Writing from a tradition that draws heavily from folklore and oral traditional arts, the novels show Morrison's critical gaze on the relevance and usefulness of these forms to carry the weight of African Americans' complex experience in the New World. Black history, that is, the ways blacks construct history, features prominently in these narratives. But it is equally fair to say that Morrison is as interested in recapturing the varied forms of African American history as she is in pushing the boundaries of oral narrative arts in light of the written tradition. In an interview with Nellie McKay, Morrison talks about her interest in recapturing the African griot tradition and recreating "something out of an old art form in [her] books" that includes an "open-ended quality" more realizable in oral performance than in the novel form (408–9).

Chapter Four

The viability of social or communal memory as alternative to hege-monic written history exists alongside its interrogation vis-à-vis class and gender tensions within the black community. The result is that one finds in Morrison's art a narrative credo that champions continued performance of that narrative in order to represent the various interests. The malleability of the spoken word, the flexibility of the text to suit audience and circum-stance, and the direct involvement of the audience in the production of the "final" text in a performance are all aspects of oral narrative aesthetics that Morrison taps into in the performance of her stories.

– FIVE –

"Singing Before the Sun Goes Down"

Jean Toomer's *Cane* and the
Black Oral Performance Aesthetic

> The folk-spirit was walking in to die on the modern desert. That spirit was so
> beautiful. Its death was so tragic. Just this seemed to sum life for me. And this
> was the feeling I put into *Cane. Cane* was a swan-song. It was a song of an end.
>
> —Jean Toomer, in Darwin Turner, *The Wayward and the Seeking*

Among writers of the Harlem Renaissance, Jean Toomer and his single full-length work, *Cane,* embody the complexities that characterized the reception of writers and works produced in the period. While Langston Hughes, speaking on behalf of his peers, declared that they "intend to express [their] individual dark-skinned selves without fear or shame" (1271), another gifted poet, Countee Cullen, expressed his displeasure on being regarded as a "Negro poet" rather than being seen simply as a poet (180). Thus, while the movement led to the production of some of the finest African American writing, it was also the period when a tragic misrepresentation of the black folk figure occurred in the craze to satiate a growing white taste for the exotic. The publication of *Cane* and Toomer's own ambivalent if not angry statements on race and the proper classification of his work quickly made Toomer and his work controversial figures.

As a preliminary gesture, I would like to address Toomer's positions on race and the reception of his work because such a consideration helps contextualize my reading of the text. *Cane* defies simple classification within the traditional genres, leading many critics to try creating a new category for the work. In addition, the fact that Toomer variously protested being classified solely as black due to the illogical basis of racial grouping in the United States created tensions in the black literary community, requiring a tedious effort to carefully separate the work from the man. Thus, it becomes useful to grasp this background completely for a fuller appreciation of the work.

American or *Black?*

Cane can be regarded as the quintessential New Negro text, judging by the varied critical comments it has received since its first publication. Charles R. Larson regards the work as *"sui generis*—a unique piece of writing in American literature as well as in the entire scope of Third World writing" (31). While the reference to "Third World" seems most bizarre, Larson's praise of the work expresses more the difficulty in placing *Cane* in any specific literary genre. For Friederike Hajek there is no doubt that Toomer, by writing *Cane,* is "one of the fathers of modern African American literature" (190). Larson's comment refers to the integrity of the text as American while Hajek confers upon Toomer the honor of being a pioneer African American artist.

An ambiguity arises, however, in the classification of both Toomer and *Cane* in the African American canon due to Toomer's own views on the matter. For the greater part of his life, Toomer vigorously resisted being called a Negro, or white, or being placed in any racial category, for that matter. In a letter to *The Liberator* written months prior to the appearance of *Cane,* Toomer described himself as "naturally and inevitably an American" with "seven blood mixtures: French, Dutch, Welsh, Negro, German, Jewish, and Indian" (Rusch, *Reader* 15). He sought to break through the prejudices attached to color and race by hailing the emergence of a new "American" race genetically and socially formed by an admixture of the previous races. Yet his position did not necessarily repudiate the basis of the conventional groups: "I am at once no one of the races and I am all of them. I belong to one of them and I belong to all" (R. Jones, *Selected Essays* 58). Toomer lived out his words, having interacted at length with blacks and whites at different points in his life. Though it does not appear that he consciously sought to be classified as white, it is highly improbable that in denying being a Negro, in 1920s America, he was not by implication claiming whiteness, what with his Caucasian physical appearance.

Despite his rejection of both categories of white and black, some of Toomer's most engaging writings, including *Cane,* celebrate black cultural consciousness. Indeed, four years before Langston Hughes's essay "The Negro Artist and the Racial Mountain" and Alain Locke's introduction to

The New Negro anthology—two essays regarded as the manifesto of the Harlem Renaissance—Toomer had started articulating some of the issues that would dominate the works of the Harlemites. One example is his essay "The Negro Emergent," where he writes, "The Negro has found his roots. He is in fruitful contact with his ancestry. He partakes of an uninterrupted stream of energy. He is moved by the vital determinants of racial heritage. And something of their spirit now lives within him. He is about to harvest whatever the past has stored, good and evil. He is about to be released from an unconscious and negative concern with it" (51). Written the year after the publication of *Cane,* his continued exposition of the unique position the Negro occupies in the American literary and cultural scene suggests that the African American experience still dominated his creative being, desperate as he was not to be called a Negro.[1]

It is a problematic position: to be possessed by the creative consciousness of a people and not desire to be part of them. In response to Toomer's ambiguous position, Rudolf P. Byrd is careful to separate the author from his creation. *Cane,* Byrd concedes, is "an American masterpiece, because it informs and illuminates, through Toomer's conscious use of Afro-American art forms, certain aspects of the Afro-American experience" (319). But Toomer, Byrd states emphatically, is not African American, and though *Cane* represents one of the finest examples of African American literature, the work, Byrd insists, "assumes or follows the racial identity of the author" (319).[2] Byrd's judgment is faulted by his extreme banishment of Toomer from the African American clan. Toomer may choose not to identify himself as black due to his own spiritual and intellectual understanding of his seven blood lines, and we may even see his response as naïve. However, to argue that *Cane* has no place in African American literary tradition is equally naïve, if not critical overkill.

No doubt, *Cane* commands equal significance in the wider American literary scene as it does in black literature, considering the connections Toomer cultivated with writers such as Sherwood Anderson and Waldo Frank. One can understand, then, why Byrd would rather praise the text in the context of non–African American tradition (even if black oral aesthetics inform its production). Besides, at the height of the Harlem Renaissance, marked by the March 21, 1924, "coming-out" party organized for a group of young black writers by Charles S. Johnson, editor of the newly formed black magazine *Opportunity,* Toomer was already out of the public scene. He had gone to the spiritual Georges I. Gurdjieff's Institute for the Harmonious Development of Man at Fontainebleau, France. It was a radical departure, so profound that in his autobiography he writes of this period thus: "I was worlds removed from the literary set. I knew little or nothing of what was happening in it. That I had once written a book called *Cain* [*sic*] seemed remote. What had happened to it I neither knew nor cared. Much less I knew of what was happening in the Negro world" (Turner, *Wayward* 131–32). No wonder that Robert C. Hart, in minimizing the influence of Toomer on the Harlem Renaissance, piquantly describes him as "a writer who passed briefly through Harlem on his way downtown and back permanently to the white world he had just left" (621).[3]

While the controversy continues over the status of Toomer and *Cane* in the black canon, other critics address issues such as gender, race, liberty, and class without necessarily connecting them to the vexatious subject. Among such critics stands Barbara Foley, whose "Jean Toomer's Washington and the Politics of Class" highlights the contradictions between Toomer's leftist ideology and his reluctance to relinquish his aristocratic privileges. Foley argues that while Toomer may have "discovered" his African American side while on a temporary teaching assignment in Sparta, Georgia, there is also "the imprint left by his consciousness of class" (290). On the other hand, Janet M. Whyde views *Cane* as part of the African American search for origins. She argues that Toomer conducts this search through the female body. Each part of the work deals with a specific inscription on the female body. In Part One, for instance, "The woman's body . . . is continually transformed into poem [*sic*]/songs in such a way that it becomes the narrative direct link to the African-American's origins" (43). Whyde's observation draws attention to such enigmatic female characters in *Cane* as Avey, Esther, Bona, and Karintha, whose "emptying of meaning" allows Toomer to "determine how and what [they] mean" (47).

Charles W. Scruggs gives the quest for meaning a mythic slant by imputing a connection between Cain, the biblical castaway, and the subject of Toomer's work. Though there is no direct reference to the figure in *Cane,* Scruggs insists, "Toomer uses Cain as a symbol of the African in a hostile land, tilling the soil of the earth, a slave, without enjoying her fruits" (278). Perhaps one quaint anomaly in Toomer's autobiographical sketches that seems to vindicate Scruggs's argument is Toomer's own use of the spelling "Cain" when referring to his work. I have already cited an example above. In that particular section, "Cain" appears seven times in six pages, and in one of the paragraphs twice (Turner, *Wayward* 127–32). Unable to explain the inconsistency, the editor, Darwin T. Turner, pronounces it an "interesting spelling error" (127). With such a frequency of usage, it is fair to surmise that the biblical figure somewhat lurked in Toomer's consciousness. In *Cane,* many of the black figures strive against unfulfilled desire: men desiring a Karintha, whose inner being they cannot understand; Kabnis, who calls himself "a dream" (81); Dan Moore ("Box Seat"), who must cut through the racial barrier set up by Muriel's nanny, Mrs. Pribby; and Tom Burwell, who is lynched in defense of his right to love a black girl ("Blood-Burning Moon"). Yet Cain, the archetypal wanderer, also bears a mark that protects him from harm,[4] which may well explain the overall exuberant mood in *Cane* as an African American work of note.

Text in Search of a Form

However viable these explorations are, to limit the interpretation of the book to its thematics hampers the full appreciation of the work. What is required is an examination that would bring the work closer to its real antecedence—the oral tradition. A performative analysis fulfills this need by noting the text's intersection between the oral culture from which it emanates and the written tradition in which that inspiration is concretized. Charles Altieri's book *Act and Quality* is relevant to my notion of performance in a literary text, especially in a "dramatistic context." According to Altieri,

> when we learn a language in a culture we develop powers to understand
> semantic properties in relation to several kinds of dramatistic contexts.
> A lexical sense of use meanings involves recognizing general scenarios
> in which the terms characteristically have force, and the pragmatics of
> speech acts gives us a framework for describing how actors in specific
> contexts can use the lexical potential of the language in order to project
> particular qualities for an audience. (55)

I am particularly interested in the emphasis Altieri places on both the reading and composition acts. Both the reader and the writer are actively involved in "the pragmatics of speech acts," and each engages the text from a dramatic angle. Altieri identifies three constituents of performance in a text, namely,

> expectations of contemplative pleasures from attending to both mimetic
> and stylistic features of a work, a readiness to become affectively engaged
> in concrete situations without the usual commitments and consequences
> that accompany emotions in ordinary experiences, and an assumption

that the text will establish in internal terms (although not exclusively so) relationships that focus one's reflections on the quality and significance of the specific actions presented. (207)

Altieri's position gives little room for an abstraction of the reading experience; however, to require the reader to be "affectively engaged in concrete situations" appeals to an aural-oral aesthetic.

Scholars such as Houston A. Baker, Jr., Frederik L. Rusch, H. William Rice, and Todd Lieber have identified certain qualities in *Cane* that make it performative. Rice, in "Two Work Songs in *Cane*," identifies song as a motif in the reading of the work. Lieber goes further to mark one of the poems in *Cane*, "Song of the Son," as the "central statement of Toomer's intentions." Then he elaborates:

The meaning of the poem hinges on the manipulation of three words: son, sun, and song. The natural sun once gave life to the "soul of slavery," but this life-giving force has almost set, and with its decline, the heritage of slavery is all but diminished, the sustenance of its tradition all but lost to the black man. The poet, however, one specific son, had embraced this heritage before the memory of it was gone completely, and by "pouring" his acceptance into art, he will make of his work a new life-giving force in the form of "an everlasting song." (181)

The historicism that Lieber attaches to the poem is noteworthy, but identifying the project as poetically inspired is even more useful. Similarly, Robert B. Jones presents *Cane* as both a lyrical novel and as metafiction because of its language structure, "narrative defamiliarization," and the way in which the work exists as an artistic reflection of the author's self (*Prison-House* 58–60). Jones's argument seems to agree with Gorham B. Munson's assessment of the overriding personality of the "narrator" in *Cane*. It is of an artist "keenly aware of life," struggling to master his craft and be in harmony with himself by viewing life in its stark reality—in other words, a "spectatorial artist" (262–63). Susan L. Blake provides a more elaborate definition of Munson's term: "For the spectatorial artist, involvement in his material means identification with his characters and recognition that the dilemma he is portraying in them is also his dilemma. The characters become more complex as they become more aware of their experience . . . as their creator . . . puts his own awareness into them" (517). With this in mind, Toomer is an artist interested in the vital dialogue between art and society, the transparent exchange that enables an artist to draw from the community as the primary source of inspiration for individual creative refinement. *Cane* is a product of such an exchange.

Jazz is another performative attribute ascribed to *Cane.* According to Frederik Rusch, "Not only does *Cane* contain jazz; its very form parallels jazz composition" (23). Similarly, Bowie Duncan describes it as "an elaborate jazz composition" (323). The cautionary remarks made in the preceding chapter regarding the fallacy in equating a written work with a musical composition still hold here; however, it is fair to regard both renditions as operating from similar compositional principles—improvisation, spontaneity, and resonance.

While Rusch and Duncan seem resolved in their classification of *Cane,* W. Edward Farrison unequivocally states what the work is not. In Farrison's opinion, *Cane* is "certainly not" a novel. Rather, "[i]t is a collection of thirteen prose sketches, fifteen occasional lyrics interspersed among them, and a closet drama. In addition there are occasional stanzas and fragments of folk verse which serve as headlines or refrains of the several prose pieces" (298–99). It is not clear what this disclaimer achieves, for neither *Cane* nor its author makes such a claim. In all his correspondence and other writings, Toomer hardly locates *Cane* in any genre. Toomer apparently conceptualized his work with the idea of capturing the various strands of black folklore in mind. The novel genre cannot sustain such a framework.

On the other hand, William L. Dutch, in a very brief essay analyzing three characters from *Cane,* succeeds in labeling the work by several genres. The stories reveal "bare essentials" like folktales; "[t]he basic structural pattern in the three character sketches is a *prose story* enclosed in a frame. The frame is a *stanza* that summarizes the story. . . . Here Toomer is making use of a literary convention used by authors of . . . *epics.* . . . Internally, the short stories or sketches are organized into sections resembling three- or four-act *dramas*" (265; emphasis added). Whether Dutch deliberately chose to mention four different genres as highlighted in the course of describing this one work is unknown, but the description points to the multigeneric credentials of *Cane* and the remarkable totality of artistic performance that distinguishes the book.

Between Farrison, who views *Cane* as merely a compendium of artistic fragments in various genres, and Dutch, who sees features of genres in the work but finds no adequate unifying term, what is missing is the obvious: that *Cane* cannot and need not be read using Western paradigms of literary appreciation. If the performance does not announce itself as such and follows a different structure, why seek a novel where there are no sufficient components of the form?

Cane operates in the context of a spoken-written interface. Black literary aesthetic comes from the interpenetration of different artistic expressions in order to make a complex and yet unified statement in a given performance. It is also based on improvisation, creativity *in situ,* and a remarkable dynamism borne by the indeterminacy of audience response in the course of a performance. What *Cane* reflects is the African American sense of unconstrained life coupled with the exuberance of artistic performance that Toomer encountered among blacks in rural Georgia.[5] It is for this reason that the majority of critics who have either sought explanations for *Cane* or dismissed its artistic merits by applying nonblack performative criteria may have continued, as Toomer lamented, "a misunderstanding in the very world, namely the literary world, in which I expected to be really understood" (Turner, *Wayward* 126).

Nevertheless, it needs stating that the choice of reading Toomer through the prism of folk aesthetics is not to suggest there is something inherently "oral" about the black experience, even if African American cultural production began from orality. As the preceding chapter makes clear, orality in itself cannot sustain a meaningful and fair representation of the various interests within the community.[6] The unresolved conflict in Morrison's *Tar Baby* between Son, the black roots-bound fugitive, and his cosmopolitan, Europhile lover, Janine, brilliantly illustrates this, for instance. The two characters are fated to endless wanderings for holding their positions unflinchingly.

It seems reasonable, then, to look elsewhere for an understanding of the oral presence in the black text. *Cane* and the other texts examined restore the oral form as primarily a tradition that has survived by its penetration into every facet of the culture so that its power lies in its omniscient presence. In other words, the value of folklore in the written medium is sustained by presenting it in its *ordinariness:* the oral performance may be a celebrated aspect of the community's cultural life, but it remains an activity that does not elicit a special demand from the community. A performance may occur as a high point of a community's festival just as it could "break out" simply at the appearance of an interested performer. As a member of the community, the artist does not necessarily ask for privileges, though the people recognize that by each performance the artist is helping them affirm their life as a community. From the songs children and adults sing as they troop out on the narrow path to the village stream to fetch water early in the morning, to the narrative poetry ("toast") performances traded among young boys in the afternoon, to the stories told at bedtime, the life of the community is marked by a continuous engagement with artistic expression in its ordinariness. This rhythm is broken only when someone who is not part of the community attempts to ill-advisedly call attention to it.[7]

When writers such as Morrison, Achebe, Soyinka, Erna Brodber, Ntozake Shange, and Heath deploy an oral voice or interrogate that voice and form, it is to ask the reader not to fetishize that tradition but to follow the artist as he or she engages the community's experience with that oral heritage. The significance of the black oral performance form in these writers' narratives is in their ability to claim the heritage and use it to make aesthetically pleasing statements. It is here that Jean Toomer's *Cane* intervenes as an African American scribal response to a dying oral literary tradition. The aesthetic that Toomer bears in his work is oral, an aesthetic that because of its pervasiveness in the text has been lost to many of its critics. In my reading of *Cane* I intend to properly situate the work within a black oral performance module and examine it as a paradigm of the interface between black spoken and written folkloric discourse.

Oral Performance and Multivocality

In his autobiography covering the year in Sparta, Toomer states the primary impetus for undertaking the *Cane* project:

> There was a valley, the valley of "Cane," with smoke-wreaths during the day and mist at night. A family of back-country Negroes had only recently moved into a shack not too far away. They sang. And this was the first time I'd ever heard the folk-songs and spirituals. They were very rich and sad and joyous and beautiful. But I learned that the Negroes of the town objected to them. They called them "shouting." They had victrolas and player-pianos. So, I realized with deep regret, that the spirituals, meeting ridicule, would be certain to die out. . . . The folk-spirit was walking in to die on the modern desert. That spirit was so beautiful. Its death was so tragic. Just this seemed to sum life for me. And this was the feeling I put into *Cane. Cane* was a swan-song. It was a song of an end. (Turner, *Wayward* 123)

Commenting on the significance of Toomer's words, Hajek states, "In writing *Cane* out of a deep sense of fundamental cultural loss, he fictionalized the historical process of that loss and thereby transcribed the waning oral tradition into a written text, preserving it as a future source of literary tradition and imagination" (190). What stands out in Toomer's statement, and in Hajek's amplification, is the explicit association Toomer makes between his literary performance and black oral tradition. Toomer's conscious articulation of this artistic impetus demands that the reading of his work take cognizance of the creative intersection between the spoken and the written word. I would further suggest that *Cane* is patterned on the aesthetics of the oral performance. By naming this pattern, we are able to unite the multiple voices that make up *Cane*.

There are reasons for applying an oral performance aesthetic to the work. First, it helps quell the continued critical speculation or puzzlement over genre. *Cane* is a written verbal performance composed as the legacy of a dying oral art; it is strange that many critics have simply ignored this fact in their search to find a genre for the work. Furthermore, a performance-based interpretation constructs the text as one coherent artistic creation rather than the fragmented work erroneously described by Farrison and others. Such a coherent reading is even more sustained in light of Toomer's refusal to have parts of the book anthologized, which to him would have "dismembered" it (Turner, *Wayward* 132). It is true that some of the stories and poems had been published earlier in magazines, but, as James Kraft rightly argues, "if it is thought that in the black aesthetic unity is organic, or self-creating, then the formal unity of *Cane* as a novel is not affected by Toomer's not originally conceiving of the parts as forming a whole" (149). Kraft's own insistence on calling the work a novel, even when he states that Toomer transforms the genre, creates a problem; but his underlying statement on the organic wholeness of the text is right on the mark.

Cane is therefore a multivocal literary accomplishment set to the music and cadence of black oral performance. Drawing from work songs and spirituals, and keenly evoking the complex cultural and political consciousness of the black folk, the textual performance exemplifies the type of synthesis that occurs when the spoken meets the written in black literary discourse. It does not matter how much value Toomer places on his Negro lineage; *Cane* demands to be read as a black text. As Houston Baker puts it, "The implicit goal of the agonized consciousness that informs Toomer's book . . . is to capture the sound of a racial soul and convert it into an expressive product equivalent in beauty and force to Afro-American folk songs, or ecstatic religious performance" (101). *Cane* is not a novel but a scribal representation of total theater that is the bedrock of black oral performance. Read thus, the pursuance of a conventional story line is a bonus; the artist and the audience are involved in a literary exchange where the story is not a story per se but an artistic *experience* drawing from the resources of the culture and the performer and appealing to the totality of the senses of the audience.

Song, as some of the critics I have mentioned above have noted, forms an important part of *Cane.* Rather than a simple motif in the text, however, song is a component of the overall aesthetic quality of the text. Sometimes the raconteur tells a story in song, in addition to the theatrical gestures. Other times music serves as strategic acoustic interventions that set up and help maintain the mood of the performance. In either case, a complementary relationship exists between the spoken word and song in the oral performance. Pointing out this interdependence in the case of the epic, Christiane Seydou states, "music and words are inextricably enmeshed; one is not subordinate to the other, rather each is superimposed on the other and each fulfills its role and unveils its part of the epic's total significance" (319). In *Cane,* there is certainly an unveiling conveyed through the agency of song, but it is not as powerful as the effect of its entrance at critical points in the text.

The generous presence of songs, balladlike narration, and poems in the text has the effect of deflecting attention to the conventions of plot—linear or convoluted. It is interesting to note how this quality remarkably pays homage to the oral performance. In *The Epic in Africa,* Okpewho notes what he perceives as the implication of a music-biased performance on the fate of the narrative's plot. He observes, "the more the music is emphasized, the less likely it is that verbal exactitude and a faultless narrative order will be observed" (57). The song might not be the text, but Toomer invests so much creative energy into the form that those who hope to find a textual unity in *Cane* based on the plot may be engaged in a futile search. By foregrounding the song, Toomer redirects the reader to the oral-aural senses that are at the center of the oral performance.

We may now appreciate the significance of "Karintha," the opening act of Toomer's performance. Toomer uses it to set the mood of the entire work. The opening song,

Her skin is like dusk on the eastern horizon,
O cant you see it, O cant you see it,
Her skin is like dusk on the eastern horizon
    . . . When the sun goes down

introduces the exuberance of a narrator who, thrilled by his privileged knowledge of the tale he is about to tell, must begin by teaching his audience lines of a song that the audience members will be invited to sing along with him as the story goes on. When Chidi Ikonne calls *Cane* "Toomer's spontaneous response to a rural black life-style" (127), the opening song certainly makes the case. The song serves as a refrain in the story, the rallying point for the narrator and his audience, occurring at the beginning, middle, and end of the story. The one at the middle appears at a crucial point of the narration, the bridge between the end of the village belle's innocence and the start of her life as a woman.

The story of a young girl who seduces all the menfolk with her "beauty, perfect as dusk when the sun goes down," is a tale of the community. From the little boy who obliges her by playing "home" with her to the preacher who condones her bad conduct, the narrator presents a community under the spell of a beauty whose inner value no one has been able to uncover. Set in Georgia, this opening story introduces a southern black community that would be delineated in a series of vignettes during the performance. The profile of the narrator is prominent here: he is a bemused artist whose lugubrious story of a misunderstood woman is only redeemed by his charming performance voice laden with irony and song ("Karintha had seen or heard, perhaps she had felt her parents loving. One could but imitate one's parents, for to follow them was the way of God" [1]).

"Men do not know that the soul of her was a growing thing ripened too soon" (2), the raconteur sings concerning Karintha. The song of an arrested development reverses in the poem "November Cotton Flower." The sudden blooming of a beautiful cotton flower amidst the cold, dry, and dead winter meets with a welcoming love more profound than the lust that greets Karintha. "November Cotton Flower" is one of two poetic performances set between "Karintha" and "Becky." The other, "Reapers," captures the rough and laborious life of the community through its harsh alliterative sounds: "Black reapers with the sound of steel on stones / Are sharpening scythes" (3). The "silent swinging" of their implement continues "one by one" without a care to the field rat killed in the process. While "Reapers" is not composed as a work song, the narration evokes an image of a labor gang working to the rhythm of a work song. This would explain why "the blade, / . . . continue[s] cutting weeds and shade" (3). A full-throated work song appears later in "Cotton Song," where, it seems, the blooming cotton in the previous poem, unlike Karintha, has naturally ripened and is ready for harvest.

A narrative anguish controls the mood of the act following the two poems. The sudden beauty of the cotton flower loved by everyone becomes a subterfuge for a community—black and white—in denial, a community whose overt religious affectations are presented as hollow when faced with an acute moral and social choice. The elegiac mode in "Becky" is punctuated by variations on a congregational phrase sermophone in the call-and-response tradition.[8] The narrator begins the story with what might be called the lyric of a song that has entered the communal lore: "Becky was the white woman who had two Negro sons. She's dead; they've gone away. The pines whisper to Jesus. The Bible flaps its leaves with an aimless rustle on her mound" (5). Like the encrypted story in the Song of Solomon of Morrison's novel, this opening bar encapsulates the narrative of a sexually active and fertile white woman rejected by both blacks and whites in her community who are embarrassed by their complicity in her misfortunes. No one claims to be the father of her two sons, and hypocritically they offer her assistance under the cover of night, ostensibly in demonstration of their Christian love.

Critical to the success of the story is the narrator's use of parallelisms and the sermophone. The latter, by implication, positions the narrator as the preacher, the moral voice of the community. He uses "we" to confess the people's meanness to Becky and her two sons, and the final moments of the story rest firmly on the narrator as the witness to the caving in of Becky's isolated cabin. The guilt of both races and their denial are presented in parallelism; so too is Becky's stony silence: "Becky had one Negro son. Who gave it to her? Damn buck nigger, said the white folks' mouth. She wouldnt tell. Common, God-forsaken, insane white shameless wench, said the white folks' mouths. . . . Who gave it to her? Low-down nigger with no self-respect, said the black folks' mouths. She wouldnt tell. Poor Catholic poor-white crazy woman, said the black folks' mouths (5)." As the story progresses, the phrases "O fly away to Jesus," "O thank y Jesus," and "O pines, whisper to Jesus" serve as sermophones emanating from the "Amen Corner" of the narrative.[9] They build to a crescendo when the narrator and Barlo, a fellow parishioner, fearing that Becky might have long died in isolation, stop at the desolate cabin. The eerie sensation of the moment is recounted with trembling, as of one telling a ghost story, and the sermophones sound more urgent:

> There was no wind. . . . Even the pines were stale, sticky, like the smell of food that makes you sick. Before we turned the bend of the road that would show us the Becky cabin, the horses stopped stock-still, pushed back their ears, and nervously whinnied. We urged, then whipped them on. Quarter of a mile away thin smoke curled up from the leaning chimney. . . . O pines, whisper to Jesus. . . . Goose-flesh came on my skin

though there still was neither chill nor wind. Uncanny eclipse! fear closed my mind. We were just about to pass. . . . Pines shout to Jesus! . . . the ground trembled as a ghost train rumbled by. (6)

The ghost train that rumbles by fells the cabin's chimney, giving the two men no opportunity to know if Becky still lives, though the narrator thinks he heard a groan from underneath the rubble (6–7).

The narrator's interest in telling the story does not lie in determining whether Becky had died earlier or because of the chimney's crash, though. The song at the beginning and end of the story suggests that whatever the circumstances of the white woman's death, her story has entered the lore of the community where it may be retold as a ghost story, performed with the heightened narrative rhetoric of a black sermon, or simply told as a legend. Toomer's interest is in the telling and its implications for the integrity of the community. By evoking the revered call-and-response tradition and showing its emptiness in the face of social discrimination, the narrator, without exculpating himself, chastises the community in their own voice. The community's false religious piety is captured by the image of the Bible that "flaps its leaves with an aimless rustle on [Becky's] mound."

Toomer changes the performance mode again from the narrative voice to the recitative in the poem "Face." Closely following "Becky," "Face" seems like a short close-up portrait of "Becky": aged, eyes filled with "mist of tears," and her muscles like "cluster grapes of sorrow / . . . / nearly ripe for worms" (8). The continuous shift in voice and mode of presentation is for dramatic effect. Sometimes involving himself in the tale, and other times taking the position of a bemused observer, *Cane*'s "narrator" achieves in a writing context some of the vocal and kinetic multiplay of the oral performer. Consider two stanzas of the poem "Cotton," where the grunts of laborers mingle with the words of this obvious work song:

Come, brother, come. Lets lift it;
Come now, hewit! roll away!
Shackles fall upon the Judgment Day
But lets not wait for it.
. . . .
Nassur; nassur,
Hump.
Eoho, eoho, roll away!
We aint agwine t wait until th Judgment Day. (9)

The onomatopoeic words create the mood of the event itself, thereby transforming the written word into an oral verbal exercise.

The transformation could be more profound. In the story "Carma," for example, the narrator combines the song mode with the speech mode, making the story told in that mode into a song in itself, before resolving the performance by a switch back to the song tone. Calling the tale he tells "the crudest melodrama" (11), the narrator alters the typical progressive layering of events in such tales by busting out in a celebratory tone. The praise reveals his keen admiration of this woman who, in overalls, "strong as any man, stands behind the old brown mule, driving the wagon home" (10). Carma's ruggedness, her sexual prowess (i.e., her ability to take on other men in the absence of her out-of-town husband), and her tricksterism blend in with the song of the wind. She obeys the "come along" song-invitation of the wind blowing through the cane leaves, and, like Brer Rabbit saving his life on the briar patch, it is among the cane stalks that Carma tricks her husband, Bane.[10]

It is also in "Carma" that the narrator makes the first direct reference to an African antecedence to his performance: "She does not sing; her body is a song. She is the forest, dancing. Torches flare . . . juju men, greegree, witch-doctors . . . torches go out. . . . The Dixie Pike has grown from a goat path in Africa" (10). Carma surrenders to the enchanting call of cane, the dominant vegetative presence, and by extension the spiritual link between Africa and the New World—the Dixie Pike and the goat path. Her evident adultery does not draw condemnation from either the community or the narrator. Though it is her feigning suicide that ultimately lands her husband in jail, the narrator's portrait of her is of a woman justified in her ways. After all, she is an embodiment of a song, a song the narrator gladly sings to the listener/reader.

I have been exploring aspects of *Cane* that suggest the need to address the work from a performative point of view. The first part of the work, which is set in rural Georgia, seems to be the segment that amply fulfills Toomer's goal in composing *Cane*. It resonates with songs and scenes that are true to African American folk culture. The story "Blood-Burning Moon" aptly concludes this section of the work with its terrifying evocation of voodoo chanting. "The full moon," Louisa deliriously realizes, is "an evil thing, an omen" that claims the life of Tom Burwell, her black suitor, lynched for daring to compete with the son of a former slave owner for her friendship (35). The words of the chant, "Red nigger moon. Sinner! / Blood-burning moon. Sinner! / Come out that fact'ry door" (35), haunt the pages of the text. For, this time, they are not chants of deliverance;

rather, they are as ominous as the full moon.[11] Harrowing as the events he recreates are, Toomer's narrator does not undercut his position as, first, a guardian of the word or, as Roger D. Abrahams, in his eponymously named work, calls the eloquent performer in the Caribbean, a "Man-of-Words." Each narrative persona in *Cane* reveals an aspect of the oral tradition and a profile of the artist as the inheritor of that tradition.

The narrative act takes on a sophisticated form when the performance moves from a rural to an urban setting. Song still reverberates in some of the stories and poems, but so do the racy and syncopated rhythms of the 1920s nascent jazz. "Seventh Street," the opening act in the middle section, aptly sets the mood of unease and yet triumphant black voice in the section: "Seventh Street is a bastard of Prohibition and the War. A crude-boned, soft-skinned wedge of nigger life breathing its loafer air, jazz songs and love, thrusting unconscious rhythms, black reddish blood into the white and whitewashed wood of Washington" (39). However, one sentence running like the major chord breaks down into a number of pauses that reel out a series of unrelated images that nevertheless make up the portrait of the vibrant and restless life of the city-dwelling African American. Amidst the larger national moral and political crises—Prohibition and the approaching World War II—the nagging question "who set you flowing?" confronts the millions of migrant African Americans from the South who people "the smooth asphalt of Seventh Street in shanties, brick office buildings theaters, drug stores, restaurants, and cabarets" (39).

Farah Jasmine Griffin best summarizes the shift in language and perspective from the first section to the second as illustrated in "Seventh Street": "We arrive from the languorous, seductive language of the South and are immediately confronted with swiftness and technology. This change in language comes as a shock to our eyes, ears, and powers of comprehension. The language confuses us and we must shift our consciousness if we are to grasp it and read its signs" (66). "Theater" is one narrative act in the middle section that reflects a vibrancy in tone and a cinematic enactment of setting. "Songs soak the wall and seep out to the nigger life of alleys and near-beer saloons," the narrator comments, still alerting us to the ubiquitous presence of song in his delineation of characters and events (50). In this act, the focus of the performer is not so much on the song as on the narrator's effort to evoke the accompanying dance.

Two major characters, John, the brother of a cabaret manager, and Dorris, a female dancer at the cabaret, are the agents through whom the narrator explores the relationship between art, liberty, and love. As the dancers rehearse with their director, John watches from the center of the theater and notes how their inner artistic abilities are being repressed by the "tame" choreographed moves led by the director. He notices Dorris, daydreams about an affair with her, then wakes up and immediately kills the desire that is the subject of his dream. On the other hand, Dorris notices John and attempts to lure him with her dance, but when "she seeks for her dance in [John's face] she finds it a dead thing in the shadow which is his dream" (53).

One major narrative quality in the story is the deep exploration of the impulses within these two characters. Internal monologues are externalized by representing each character's thoughts on paper as if they were a written dramatic script. The gulf between the thoughts racing through the mind of John and his failure to pursue what would have been a fusion of his artistic mind with Dorris's artistic body is represented through a set of dualisms (we will ignore the obvious gender stereotypes Toomer plays up here). The theater lights cast a symbolic streak on John that leaves his face part orange and part shadow; the narrator informs us that "John's body is separate from the thoughts that pack his mind" (50). John possesses a powerful creative force that he transmits to others, even to inanimate objects. As he enters the theater, the walls, described as "sleeping singers," "start throbbing to a subtle syncopation. And the space-dark air grows softly luminous" (50). As he watches the women at the rehearsal, mixed feelings of sadness and artistic exuberance fill his consciousness: "John: Soon the director will herd you, my full-lipped, distant beauties, and tame you, and blunt your sharp thrusts in loosely suggestive movements, appropriate to Broadway. (O dance!) Soon the audience will paint your dusk faces white, and call you beautiful. (O dance!) Soon I . . . (O dance!) I'd like . . ."(50). The parenthetical exclamations represent artistic talent crying for release. The jazz pianist in the theater performs improvisations that beg for an equally unrestricted interpretation through dance. The elliptical sentences cited above, however, reveal John's fear of claiming what he desires.

Toomer portrays Dorris as responding to the freedom call of jazz music. To catch John's attention in order to establish sexual love between them, she lets loose the stream of her dancing energy that even her director cannot control as he suspends further practice of his monotonous steps. And the narrator exults in her artistic triumph:

Dorris dances. She forgets her tricks. She dances.
Glorious songs are the muscles of her limbs.
And her singing is of canebrake loves and mangrove feastings. (52–53)

"Theater" does not simply portray cabaret life. It is Toomer's effort at evoking the gamut of emotions and spectacle readily realizable in oral performance. Through the narrator, Toomer animates the sights, sounds, and inner ruminations of the actors so that the audience may experience the emotional intensity of the moment. Suddenly, the inner libidinous consciousness jumps onto the pages to the unflagging jazz music, and a dancing body yearns for a like mind. The story ends with a disappointed Dorris, but what will continue to echo is the throbbing beat of the piano and the image of "Glorious Dorris" who "whirls, whirls, dances" (53).

There is also the sense of the dramatic in *Cane*. Some of the stories in the middle section show a copious amount of attention to the mannerisms and gestures of the characters. The unexpected shout of "JESUS WAS ONCE A LEPER!" by Dan Moore at the theater ("Box Seat" 66) and the eloquent speech Paul makes to the black doorman at the club where he had gone on a tension-filled date with Bona, a white woman (78) are powerful dramatic moments in the text. The sustained dialogues between characters also suggest the dramatic character of the stories.

It is, however, in "Kabnis" that Toomer invests his finest dramatic resources. Darwin T. Turner, in his introduction to an edition of *Cane*, calls "Kabnis" a "novelette-drama" (xxi). The reason for Turner's quaint naming is not difficult to see. "Kabnis" is divided into six parts (or acts); extensive scene and character portraits lace the dialogues. The first act flows completely as Kabnis's stream of consciousness or internal monologue. From the second part onward, the narrative develops in a dramatic format as Kabnis interacts with other characters in the text. Yet a hyphenated name for "Kabnis," or any other part of *Cane*, is not necessary. The fluidity of oral performance observed by the artist's ability to move across a range of expressive forms equally applies to the text.

"Kabnis" represents a maturation of the narrative effort begun in the earlier stories where a deep psychological exploration of the characters leads to a greater specificity in the way in which the narrators attribute words to the individual characters. I have already noted an instance of this in "Theater," where the thoughts of John and Dorris are presented as if they were engaged in a spoken dialogue. The same style is evident in "Box Seat," where Dan's and Muriel's thoughts are also presented in a script format. As can be observed from Okpewho's field documentation, the drama form offers the best style for the rendition of an oral performance.[12] It offers a visual representation of the "democratization" that characterizes the narrative process; while members of the audience expect the performer to exercise the leading role in the realization of the performance, both they and the artist know that the enactment is as much their own making as the artist's.

Though no live audience exists in a writing context, Toomer creates a sense of immediacy in "Kabnis" through an elaborate description of the setting and characters. One such vivid description relates to Lewis, a black man from the North who is apparently on a politically inspired familiarization visit to the South. The following commentary precedes his first speech in the performance: "Lewis enters. He is the queer fellow who has been referred to. A tall wiry copper-colored man, thirty perhaps. His mouth and eyes suggest purpose guided by an adequate intelligence. He is what a stronger Kabnis might have been, and in an odd faint way resembles him" (95). Here Toomer combines a description of Lewis's physical features with a commentary on his significance; Lewis is a counterfoil to Kabnis, a failed teacher and poet in search of reconciliation with his past and present.

Despite the effort to write the dialogues in everyday African American vernacular, "Kabnis" presents moments of sheer poetic brilliance. For instance, nightlife in Sempter, the play's setting, is described with sensuous tenderness to reveal the beauty of the rural South: "Night, soft belly of a pregnant Negress, throbs evenly against the torso of the South. Night throbs a womb-song to the South. Cane-and cotton-fields, pine forests, cypress swamps, sawmills, and factories are fecund at her touch. Night's womb-song sets them singing" (103). Poetic excursions such as this in the midst of everyday prose make *Cane* a testimony to the multiple levels of verbal ability an artist working with a black oral performance aesthetic can accomplish.

There is no doubt that the problematic position Toomer assumed in relation to his race places a serious burden on the acceptance of his work into the African American literary tradition. Having at certain times denied his blackness, to call *Cane* an African American text becomes somewhat like an appropriation. However, so much blackness is invested in the integrity of the text that it is impossible to ignore its place in fashioning a new African American literary voice, especially in light of the Harlem Renaissance. Besides, there is not much value in playing identity politics by insisting that a writer's racial identity is the precondition for determining where the writer's work belongs.

Cane's artistic brilliance emanates from its indebtedness to the oral culture experienced by the author during his short stay in rural Georgia. The work portrays black experience from a perspective that neither glamorizes nor debases it. Toomer has stated that his two primary aims for writing are to "essentialize" and "spiritualize" experience (R. Jones, *Selected Essays* 44). This is certainly true in *Cane* where the beauty of black life, its harsh and not so winsome experience, and the deep religious heritage of the African American, so powerfully expressed in song, are masterfully represented.

I am suggesting that applying the aesthetics of black oral performance offers a more robust approach to its artistic appreciation. By performance, I mean the exchange that occurs between an oral performer and his or her audience as well as the vivid evocation of the context of interaction. The value does not lie merely in the text the artist performs but in the totality of verbal and nonverbal effects that come into play in the course of the act. In fact, the entire artistic experience *is* the performance. The individual creativity and talent that the performer brings into that exchange are part of the performance's text, as well as the cultural knowledge and sense of the community's aesthetics against which the audience judges the performer.

By applying the aesthetics of the African oral performance to *Cane,* a reconciliation of the various parts of the text that few critics have tried to glean becomes possible. Toomer presents himself (sometimes through his narrative surrogates) as a guardian of the word, the oral performer who seems to exult in the thrill of displaying the breadth of his folk artistry. In addition, a performance approach enables us to invoke the concept of the multigenre that is at the heart of the oral performance.[13] Far from being a compartmentalization of artistic resources, the oral text thrives in the fluidity by which artistic expression, time, and space travel and interact.

There is also the matter of spoken-written interface in *Cane.* Toomer writes that he composed *Cane* as a "swan-song" for a black oral culture he saw slowly dying. The transposition of that culture to print is not literal. *Cane* contains poems composed as songs, but we cannot hear them aurally. What we derive is a *sense* of the songs, the oral ambiance of their composition. They are composed in the *spirit* of the oral performance. *Cane* certainly benefits from the written tradition, but Toomer suspends certain conventions of writing to accommodate the oral.

Cane, therefore, exemplifies a superb blending of the African American oral aesthetic with the written tradition. It does not borrow from the oral tradition; rather, it manifests that tradition. Instead of being a swan-song, the book is a performance that demonstrates the resilience of the oral tradition in adapting to changing times and space: from Africa to the New World; from the effervescence and immediacy of the spoken word to the durable print tradition. While its author may choose to construct new identities for himself, as the times compel, *Cane* demands to be read as a black text, a fine example of the interface between writing and oral traditional aesthetics.

— AFTERWORD —

Of Goat Paths and Dixie Pike

In the preceding pages, I have followed an interpretive model for reading the selected Afro-diasporic narratives that emphasizes their folkloric content. I began by placing the texts as folkloric acts based on their indebtedness to black folk culture in form and meaning. My inquiry is framed by the discussion of the relationship between the spoken and the written word in Afro-diasporic narratives. Folklore is a viable form for such an inquiry because of its direct connection to the community's sense of well-being and its capacity to register the transformations that occur within the group. Both the Old World's oral tradition and the artistic forms available or fashioned in the Americas find expression in the Afro-diasporic novel.

In exploring the interface between the oral and the written in the Afro-diasporic narrative, I have argued that such an inquiry must move beyond the practice of identifying folkloric materials in the texts. It is not enough to show how indebted they are to the oral tradition. In my study, I have shown that the written narrative is a folkloric act. I have also adopted a way of reading the texts that reveals the significance of folklore to their success as creative endeavors.

The inspiration for this project came about many years ago when I came across an anthology of Guyanese mythic figures and read the entry for Coolie Jumbie. Coolie Jumbie is a spirit that prowls around cemeteries and confronts unsuspecting passersby with a wide grin, saying, "Ever see teet' as dese?" as it exposes a frightening jagged dentition made up of metals, broken bottles, and pins. I was shocked. Years before I read that book, while in middle school in Nigeria, some of us would ask one of the guards in the boarding school I attended to tell us stories. De John, one of the three security men who worked the night shift, always obliged. He walked with a limp and we always wondered how he would cope if he had to chase an intruder on foot. Because it was late at night, often after regulation time, he always chose to tell creepy stories—infants crying in the bushes only to gobble up the unsuspecting adult who rushed in sympathy to save the child; beautiful women standing by the roadside who turned out to be just skeletons, using one of their ancient bones to crush the head of the unfortunate lover; men who were actually women and seemed to enjoy inflicting pain on the opposite sex. De John was full of stories with gloomy endings, and this elementary school dropout in his late fifties regaled us with those stories for years to come in boarding school.

A few weeks before our high school graduation, I remember De John telling us a special story. He said it was a true story of an incident that happened to him and that he wanted to use it to explain his fascination with ghost stories. He was in his early twenties, he said, and had a job as a driver for an executive in an oil company in Port Harcourt, a city about an hour away from where our school was located. He enjoyed the benefit of taking the car home and reporting at the executive's home early each morning. On this one day, it was approaching midnight before he started home. On the way home, there was this long stretch of road where nobody lived. It was in that area that De John told us he beheld a terrible sight. On the roadside was the body of a man lying spread-eagled with eyes wide open and mouth in a wide grin that exposed his full front teeth. It was when he stopped by the body that he saw that they were not human teeth but an assortment of broken bottles in jagged positions. One glimpse at the body and he quickly sped away in dread.

Five minutes later, he saw a young woman carrying a sack on her head flagging down his approaching car. De John could not imagine what the woman could be doing on the road at that hour of the night, but he was so grateful for the prospect of human company that he pulled up to where the woman stood. She got in after putting the sack in the trunk of the car and De John, without prompting, began telling the woman about the frightful sight he had just witnessed. The woman did not say a word but kept nodding her head as she kept her eyes straight on the road. De John described the ghastly grin on the man's face and told her how he had never seen a mouth full of broken bottles in place of teeth. Immediately, the woman turned to De John and, wide eyed, said, "*Abi na like dis?*"[1] She opened a wide mouth revealing rows of sharp objects, needles, nails, and pieces of broken bottles that stood where teeth should be. According to De John, right there the woman's face was transformed to that of the man on the road. De John screamed and in fear swerved off the road and hit a tree trunk. The woman had vanished immediately after she revealed her true self. De John could not say how he managed to get home, but once he recovered, he quit his job in the city and returned to the village. From his story, we found out that his bad leg was because of the injury he sustained on that fateful night.

After finding out about Coolie Jumbie, it became clear to me that De John had constructed a grand narrative scheme for his young graduating audience. His fateful encounter embodied all the horror stories he had streamed into our consciousness up to that moment—that is, before I found out that the dead and living wo/man he met on the road was no other than Coolie Jumbie, hanging around the cemeteries and the consciousness of the Guyanese since the era of slavery when those harried Africans made the Middle Passage. De John wanted to make sure that by the time we graduated, he was no longer just the teller of ghost stories; he was in fact the text of a ghost story. For his final performance to the graduates, he probably felt that the ultimate tale had to be him, not him telling us about fictive characters and their vicissitudes.

Encountering Roy Heath's novels in college, reading about Kwaku and Bakoo confirmed to me that the relationship between Africa and blacks in the diaspora was not a mere academic exercise, unlike the sense one gets in considering Paul Gilroy's "Black Atlantic." The linkages are real, making it imperative that studies exploring the dimensions of diaspora consciousness be sustained and pursued with the seriousness and commitment that the subject deserves. I offer this book in the spirit of such a pursuit. It is also written to extend the frontiers of folklore studies. Conducting fieldwork and documenting oral traditions and performances for analysis are useful. But my work attempts to use the insight gained from such folklore studies to conduct literary analysis of texts that suggest that they would yield deeper meaning through that prism.

In all the texts examined in this study, I have focused on their status as folkloric performances. In these works, the connection to the oral tradition is not a question of borrowing. The texts do not embody elements of folk culture; rather, they are unique folkloric acts. Through the written word, the mythic or folkloric sign is intensified. Writing is the context of performance. Thus, a performative approach to criticism of black texts is crucial to the formulation of a viable black aesthetic.

Furthermore, Harris, Heath, Morrison, and Toomer, in their respective works, offer unique representations of the interface between the spoken and the written. Be it the resuscitation of mythic figures as agents of hope and (inter)national redemption in Harris or Heath, or Morrison's playful narrator in *Jazz* and Toomer's exuberant raconteur, these writers have broadened the area of interaction between the two communicative forms. What this research advocates is that readers and critics of Afro-diasporic narratives must become aware of the nature of the oral-written interface and respond with a commensurate emphasis on the texts as performances.

In the chapters on Morrison and Toomer, I have emphasized the texts as performances by examining how the authors construct their narrative voices and imitate some of the performance nuances identifiable in an oral context. Heath and Harris, on the other hand, have so integrated folklore or the mythic sign into their works that a proper understanding of their narratives can hardly be achieved unless one understands their grammar of meaning.

The interrogation of the oral form through writing, most noticeable in works by Morrison and Harris, is a vital aspect of sustaining the tradition. Indeed, in the oral performance, the skill of an artist is partly assessed by the extent to which he or she has extended the frontiers of the tradition. When these writers problematize some aspects of the oral tradition, it is for making them more usable and relevant for contemporary audiences. Consider, for example, the envisioning of hope in Guyana. From the uncertainty and fear inherent in the myth of Bakoo, Heath delineates a persona (Kwaku) who, though conscious of his vulnerability, is able to project a Guyanese personality at peace with his environment, thereby offering hope for a nation in political flux. Thus, Heath seems to be making the argument that myth is the society's hope.

Folklore largely reflects every community's cultural consciousness. The New World black "community" is no exception. Because of historical circumstances, the African diasporic written narrative carries an artistic heritage composed of oral and written forms. The task facing the critic is to account for both forms adequately. What this study has done is focus on that creative space where the oral meets the written and interpret the texts as full-fledged performances helping to vitalize the black aesthetic.

– Notes –

Chapter One

1. One of the dangers inherent in the Afrocentric ideology is that it has the possibility of articulating a philosophy of homogeneity that effaces the peculiar experiences of blacks in the New World, as against Africa.

2. This point on defining aesthetics in geocultural terms is driven home in a dialogue between Achebe and Baldwin. While Achebe argues that aesthetics stems from "art which is committed to people," Baldwin interprets Achebe's position as pointing to morality. "And beneath that word [morality]," Baldwin states, "we are confronted with the way we treat each other. That is the key to any morality." As an African, Achebe's definition is informed by anticolonial struggle, whereas racial equality and tolerance are at the heart of Baldwin's point of view, being an African American. See Dorothy Randall-Tsuruta, "In Dialogue to Define Aesthetics: James Baldwin and Chinua Achebe," 214, 216.

3. On the other hand, a peremptory denial of a connection between Africa and blacks in the New World is absurd. This is the case with C. L. R. James's surprising response when asked about the connection of the African Caribbean to Africa in an interview with Alder Calder. His words: "I do not know what are the African roots of the language and culture of Caribbean intellectuals. I am not aware of the African roots of my use of the language and culture. I pay a lot of respect to Africa. I have been there many times. I have spoken to many Africans. I have read their literature. But we of the Caribbean have not got an African past. We are black in the skin, but the African civilisation is not ours. The basis of our civilisation in the Caribbean is an adaptation of Western civilisation" ("An Audience with C. L. R. James" 6). Significantly, though, see also chapter 7 of Kenneth Ramchand's pioneering work *The West Indian Novel and Its Background*, where he traces African presence in early West Indian texts.

4. There is ample data on the most common slave sources in Africa, but

Gwendolyn Midlo Hall's *Slavery and African Ethnicities in the Americas* is perhaps the most comprehensive in providing detailed data on the ethnic identities of many of the Africans sold into slavery. Critically, the information is gleaned from the direct identifications by the slaves. According to her, "We [African diaspora scholars] can no longer be satisfied with simplistic, romanticized ideas about the identities of the African ancestors of African Americans" (165). Hall's work is an impressive piece of data mining and compelling findings on the subject.

5. For example, in Ngugi wa Thiong'o's novels, one observes a consistency in his narrators' efforts at securing group solidarity. Similarly, the proverbs that appear as linguistic and thematic capsules in Achebe's narratives effectively place the narrative consciousness within the ethical and aesthetic consciousness of the Igbo community. The same cultural affinity between the writer and community can be observed in writings by Buchi Emecheta, Wole Soyinka, Sembene Ousmane, and Ama Ata Aidoo, among others.

6. See texts as varied as J. Nozipo Maraire's *Zenzele: A Letter for My Daughter*, *Bones* by Chenjarai Hove, and Nurrudin Farah's *Maps*.

7. Part of the theory Henry Louis Gates formulates in *The Signifying Monkey*, and which informs the analysis of some African American texts found in the second part of his book, is based on these two stylistic devices of the black plantation society.

8. As an instructor in courses where I have black students from the Caribbean as well as the United States, I have not failed to notice how, say, a Jamaican student would express disgust with what she perceives as unacceptable conduct by "Americans," by which she means blacks and whites of the United States.

9. In *The Black Atlantic* Gilroy describes the West as stepparents of blacks (49).

10. In his recent work *Confluences: Postcolonialism, African American Literary Studies, and the Black Atlantic*, John Cullen Gruesser praises Gilroy's work for its use of postcolonial theoretical terminology in the study of African diasporic literature. Gruesser concedes that Gilroy's approach is useful to "a lesser extent [to] African philosophy, music, literature, and political discourse" (17) than to diasporic Africans. Although Gruesser proceeds to study African American literature in light of Gilroy's Black Atlantic, it is ironic that a concept that serves to place Africa at the periphery (Black Atlantic) appropriates some terminologies by which the vast majority of scholars and writers from Africa engage the cultural production in the continent (postcolonial studies).

11. See Jack Goody, *The Interface Between the Written and the Oral*, 32.

12. See, for example, Goody's *Domestication of the Savage Mind*, where "savage" connotes "inferior," "unlettered," and "primitive."

13. See also Christopher Wise's essay "Nyama and Heka: African Concepts of the Word," where he offers a comprehensive study of the complex relationship between the West African griot's abilities and the Mande term "Nyama," loosely translated as occult abilities (19, 26). One of the critical observations Wise makes in his analysis is the inseparability of the griot's occult power and the spoken/ aspirated word. Through in-depth etymological research, Wise's study seeks to reestablish an African approach to language that locates creative force, seat of consciousness, and ontological outlook in the spoken word, especially the kind embodied in and made manifest by the griot.

14. Isidore Okpewho's essay "The Cousins of Uncle Remus" is a critical response to Roberts's *Trickster to Badman*. There Okpewho cautions that an overemphasis on the African roots of African American creative imagination could wrongly misstate the genius of the African American artist. In his words, "we do not give proper credit to Afro-American genius if we put all our investigative energy into tracing to African sources every cultural achievement it has recorded" (27).

Chapter Two

1. In his study of the epic and novel genres, M. M. Bakhtin lists three features that distinguish the novel from other narrative forms. Among them is the novel's contemporaneity: "the zone of maximal contact with the present . . . in all its openendedness" (11). By using this criterion Bakhtin sees the world of the epic as closed, "walled from all subsequent times," and therefore lacking space for "any openendedness, indecision, indeterminacy" (16). One must add that Bakhtin's distinction is not entirely applicable to the African epic where, due to the interaction between the singer and the audience, the performance is never a closed text; the experience it evokes may belong to a heroic past, but the performance consciously addresses itself to the concerns of the contemporary or immediate audience.

2. Webb's study also uses the theory of "magical realism" in reading the novels. Many scholars have applied this concept while examining Caribbean writing, or Latin American writing, to be specific. It operates on recognizing mystery as part of material consciousness. But while this term is consistent with Webb's argument, Selwyn R. Cudjoe rejects the implications of the term "magical" since it seems to suggest that an experience represented by such a term is not historical or real. In the place of magical or marvelous realism, he proffers "critical realism," because novels under this rubric that "attempt to discover the 'essence' of Caribbean experience . . . contain social analyses of that reality" (265). Cudjoe's argument is pertinent especially when he uses it to repudiate the idea of history as cyclical. The Caribbean experience writers represent, he asserts, "proceeds forward in an opening or spiral development which is neither magical nor cyclical" (265).

3. See further discussion of the phenomenon in Wilson Harris's discourse on trance in Voodoo religion in the next chapter.

4. I am referring to Soyinka's exposition on the Ogun's mythopoesis in his essay "The Fourth Stage," where he describes the abyss into which Ogun descends to fashion a bridge between Yoruba deities and mortals as the "seething cauldron of the dark world will and psyche, the transitional yet inchoate matrix of death and becoming" (*Myth* 142).

5. André Breton's definition of surrealism as the "psychic automatism in its pure state, by which one proposes to express—verbally, by means of the written word, or in any other manner—the actual functioning of thought" aptly captures the mood of this moment in the novel (*Manifestoes* 26).

6. One of the character flaws of the trickster figure is its habit of overreaching itself. Most times, it manifests when the trickster, in the height of a momentary success or achievement, makes a spontaneous boast that it quickly realizes would be difficult to fulfill. The trickster embodies this flaw and it forms the trope of

the trickster's adversities. In Kwaku's case, there is complexity in the title; not to keep his mouth shut seems to point to Bakoo's restlessness and reflects the trickster's inevitable "failing."

Chapter Three

1. One tendency among Caribbean writers is their use of classical mythology alongside African symbols; Derek Walcott, Orlando Patterson, and Harris readily come to mind. Figures such as Poseidon, Sisyphus, Tiresias, and Odysseus appear in their narratives as archetypes of the Caribbean situation. A simple way to explain the presence of these classical mythic figures in Caribbean writing is to see it as the manifestation of the colonial experience. But it is not so simple; Harris, for example, argues for a cross-cultural consciousness, a consciousness that embodies the mythology of all the groups that constitute Caribbean society. Also, in his typology, the inclusion of these classical figures does not necessarily guarantee that they retain their original symbolism; their symbolism is more likely to be reversed or subverted in order to make room for a new thinking. The relevance of a cross-cultural consciousness, as Wilfred Cartey suggests, is to "give credence to the transformative vision that leads to new formations, new possibilities, to a new presence" (402). It is this search for newness that might explain the use of African, Amerindian, and European mythologies in delineating Caribbean experience.

2. This definition is by no means limited to the present discussion. See, for instance, Joel Adedeji's assertation about the aesthetic principle governing Yoruba theater: "The aesthetics of the Yoruba theater are the total integration, the gestalt of all the art forms in one performance" (63). What he states here for the Yoruba of Nigeria can also be said of several other African societies.

3. Wole Soyinka is a major proponent of this position. In *Myth, Literature and the African World,* a book that best articulates Soyinka's theory of African literature, his characterization of African ritual theater seems overly "spiritual" and does not appear to give much attention to the secular and artistic dimensions of this theater. Artistic effects such as lighting, the motions of the performers, and verbal resources are seen as props to "control and render concrete, to parallel . . . the experiences or intuitions of man in that far more disturbing environment which he defines variously as void, emptiness or infinity" (39–40). While this interpretation is mostly valid, especially for an understanding of the ritual archetype, it undervalues the significance of these resources as celebratory of the performers' creative genius.

4. In her reading of Masters, Hena Maes-Jelinek identifies these two lives of the character, but notes, too: "As a matter of fact, Masters experiences several deaths and resurrections, each of which makes possible his and the narrator's understanding of yet another slice of experience and casts a different light on, or even undermines, the previous one" (*Labyrinth of Universality* 302). It is true, though, that the first and second appearances are the crucial ones.

5. The partial image could relate to Antonio Benitez-Rojo's conceptualization of the Caribbean text as "a consummate performer, with recourse to the most daring improvisations to keep from being trapped within its own textuality" (29).

In each instance (i.e., Harris's and Benitez-Rojo's), what is emphasized is a resistance to closure.

6. Harris's description of Weyl's death bears an uncanny similarity with Soyinka's description of Sekoni's death in his novel *The Interpreters*. Like Weyl, Sekoni, an engineer, is one of the five protagonists in the novel who fight a corrupt government establishment. Sekoni constructs a power grid that offers a cheaper source of electricity to a rural community, but his work is dismissed as junk so that an expatriate's alternative could be purchased, with the establishment receiving a bribe before signing the contract. Sekoni suffers a mental breakdown as a result. He resigns his position and, on a fateful rainy night, while driving his car, he fails to see an oncoming vehicle that has lost control and is crushed to death. Soyinka, in a passage laden with images of sacrifice, writes: "The rains of May become in July slit arteries of the sacrificial bull, a million bleeding punctures of the sky-bull hidden in convulsive cloud humps, black, overfed for this one event, nourished on horizon tops of endless choice grazing, distant beyond giraffe reach. . . . The Dome cracked above Sekoni's short-sighted head one messy night. Too late he saw the insanity of a lorry parked right on his path, a swerve turned into a skid and cruel arabesques of tyres. A futile heap of metal, and Sekoni's body lay surprised across the open door" (155).

7. Maes-Jelinek views this ability as indicative of Harris's idea of comedy ("'Carnival'" 49). Her argument seems to depend on the novel's use of Dante's Inferno in *Divine Comedy* as a motif. To regard the novel as a comedy may be a stretch on the form, though she rightly notes how the interchange of masks by the characters "unravel[s] deeply buried and unconscious residues of individual and historical experience" (49).

8. Aware of the close affinity between his erasure of the author-character divide and postmodern declaration of the death of the author, Harris makes the following distinction between his technique and postmodernism: "Now I happen to know that some post-modernists would claim that they too advance this notion that the author can be erased from the text. At a certain level I agree with this, but at another level I diverge from it profoundly because in my case, what I am saying is that when the author ceases to be the kind of realistic author which one usually looks for, what one is breaking is the authoritarian model, the author becomes himself a fiction created by his own characters, the authoritarian model is broken and in breaking it, one has become susceptible to a tradition which one has apparently lost" ("Literacy and the Imagination" 82). That openness on the author's part to lost traditions, to be a channel through which a "lost" tradition "*returns* [and] *nourishes us even though it appears to have vanished*," is the literate imperative (ibid., 86; original emphasis).

9. There is also a biblical antecedent to the classical version of the serpent staff. As Moses leads the Israelites through the wilderness, the people complain about the hardships on the way. God sends fiery serpents to bite the complaining people and many die. But Moses intercedes on behalf of the people and God relents by directing Moses to make a bronze serpent and place it on a staff that those who are bitten and look at the bronze serpent may live (Numbers 21:4–9). The narrative's promise of life available through the inanimate staff certainly coheres with Harris's latter-day construct.

10. See Harris's more recent work *The Dark Jester,* where Jest is also evoked as the primary medium for retrieving the buried history of Atahualpa, an Inca ruler who was deposed and executed by the Spanish colonial Francisco Pizarro. Living almost exclusively from the "City of Dream" (39), the narrator depends on the Jester as guide. "Jest," the epigraph notes, "is miraculously potent in the most serious of arts which depict reverses in accepted habit in exploring the enigmas of universality" (ix).

11. Even the attribution of "W. H." to Harris is at best an effort on my part to establish a relationship between the name on the cover of the text and the authorship of the work. It is as likely that they are Harris's initials as it is coincidental that both entities share similar name initials. I think that Harris's interest in exploring multiple identities of his characters and the construct of the "Dreambook" could possibly account for this deliberate ambiguity.

12. "Horrow Lives On," *Time* (December 11, 1978): 28.

13. Genesis 28:10–12.

14. See also Harris's essay "Closing Statement: Apprenticeship to the Furies," where he contends that the "mystery of consciousness" demands moving away from "one-track realism" and forging new texts that "must . . . of necessity seek to cross chasms in reality [and] cross the familiar raw material of existence we would associate with a mere blackboard, for instance, to an element such as a storm or a wave upon which the elements write with the chalk of lightning" (248).

15. See Soyinka's *Myth,* where he presents an African ontology that aligns perfectly with Harris's. Note especially chapter 2, "Drama and the African World-view" (37–60). It is worth stating, however, that in this work Soyinka appears to overstate Yoruba spirituality whereby this particular worldview is offered as a prototype of African traditional religions and worldviews. It is also debatable whether all African societies spiritualize their theater and arts in the way he argues here.

16. In the Gospel according to John, Jesus raises Lazarus from the dead (John 11:1–44).

17. Harris invests considerable space in deploying carnival tropes in this novel, and in this, his extensive use of carnival reflects what J. Michael Dash describes as a "tempting" part of Caribbean aesthetics because "it so obviously facilitates an exploration of a free flow of time and space as well as the permutations, randomness, and eclecticism that are central to the cultural diversity of the Americas" (128). *Jonestown* elaborately utilizes this metaphor.

18. Harris makes a similar point in his talk titled "Literacy and the Imagination," where he states: "It is very easy for a society to overturn an oppressor, but it is equally easy for those who overturned the oppressor to become the oppressor in turn. If one polarizes the world dreadfully, the oppressor and the oppressed, then one is no longer in a position to understand who the oppressor is, how he relates to one, who the oppressed are, how the oppressed relate to one. To understand that, one has to rehearse the implications" (85).

Chapter Four

1. Although not without its critics, on May 21, 2006, the *New York Times Book*

Review selected Morrison's novel *Beloved* as "the single best work of American fiction published in the last 25 years." http://www.nytimes.com/2006/05/21/books/fiction-25-years.html?ex=1156046400&en=f902fa6a21921563&ei=5070.

2. See Elmar Lehmann's article "Remembering the Past: Toni Morrison's Version of the Historical Novel" and Justine Tally's "Reality and Discourse in Toni Morrison's Trilogy: Testing the Limits" for instances of this historical linearity attached to the named novels.

3. This connection receives full play in Morrison's series of lectures on American cultural history, *Playing in the Dark: Whiteness and the Literary Imagination.* See especially chapter 1: "Black Matters," where she outlines the dimensions of the unspoken relationship.

4. See Gates's *The Signifying Monkey,* where he argues that the trope of the "Talking Book" is the "ur-text" of African American narrative tradition (xxv, 127–69).

5. To his credit, John N. Duvall's biocritical work on the early novels of Morrison avoids this fallacy in his study of the connections between Morrison and William Faulkner. The goal is not to "measure Morrison on the yardstick of a Faulkner," Duvall states; instead, by examining the intertextuality, "one can validly read not only Faulkner's influence on Morrison, but also Morrison's influence on Faulkner—how her fiction and literary criticism may cause one to rethink Faulkner in a fundamental way" (75).

6. Since I am interested in examining Morrison's performance of African American folklore in her novels, I have tried to steer away from exploring other aspects of her writing. Certainly, there is validity to an "Americanist" reading of Morrison. Historically, both black and white and, indeed, all the other races have, through their unique cultural traditions, combined to form what is termed American literature. Thus, such readings of Morrison that have tried to show Morrison's contribution to or place in the American literary tradition are legitimate. However, one must be ready to scrutinize such explorations to identify whose purpose is served, as Morrison's remark enjoins.

7. One problem with Lipsitz's definition, however, is that the history he identifies as emanating from this counter-memory is still lineal, even though he sees it as "supplying new perspectives about the past" (162).

8. April Lidinsky's essay "Prophesying Bodies: Calling for a Politics of Collectivity in Toni Morrison's *Beloved*" vigorously discusses the collectivity of rememory in this novel. Beyond the connection Paul D and Sethe make through their common experience, Lidinsky notes that communal rememory also "dissolves power's vertical compartmentalization of knowledge, temporality and identities" (207).

9. Ashraf H. A. Rushdy correctly places the emphasis on Milkman's inward journey rather than the economic quest when he asserts, "Milkman begins his odyssey putatively in search of this bag of gold, but this gold has been transmuted. What Milkman seeks is family knowledge" (315). Compare with the argument Marianne Hirsch makes in "Knowing Their Names," where she sees Milkman's gold hunt as gender-determined when contrasted with Pilate's motive for keeping the bag (83).

10. This reading of Pilate's figure in the novel warrants emphasis because it challenges a tendency among some literary critics of the book to overstate her

image as the spiritual life force in the narrative. Gayl Jones, for instance, calls her the novel's "fount of fantastic imagery" (172). There is no doubt that among the living Dead family, Pilate is a contrast to the materialistic and self-centered attitude of her relatives; however, once this attribute is placed within the larger context of the novel's engagement with the notion of history, its significance is radically diminished.

11. Morrison certainly has a personal investment in this incident and its ramifications in the novel. In an interview with Cecil Brown, she reveals that her mother did not have a birth certificate, while her aunt had one that did not bear her name but simply the racial description, "Negro Child" (461).

12. In contrast with the genealogy of Macon's name, consider how he, still illiterate, names his daughter Pilate. The younger Macon recalls how his father, in grief after losing his wife in childbirth, "had thumbed through the Bible, and since he could not read a word, chose a group of letters that seemed to him strong and handsome; saw in them a large figure that looked like a tree hanging in some princely but protective way over a row of smaller trees" (18). Faced with what seems an impossible task, he imposes his tactile and imaginative abilities on the lifeless letters, freely associating his known world as a farmer with the simple shapes of the alphabet.

13. W. Lawrence Hogue, in *Race, Modernity, Postmodernity,* interprets the relationship between Solomon, Milkman, and the question of flight in terms of gender. Milkman's "discovery" of his ancestral line, Lawrence argues, though celebratory of African oral historical tradition, nevertheless "reflects a social order grounded in phallocentricism, his own egocentricism, and Western logocentricism" (44). The song that preserves the account of Solomon's flight represents this social order and does not glorify the patriarch since it is actually "a voice that bemoans . . . loss" (44). In other words, Solomon liberates himself at the expense of his wife, Ryna, and children, including Jake (Macon Dead). Trudier Harris makes a similar case when she asserts, "The celebration of flying simultaneously highlights Ryna's insanity and the fatherlessness of Solomon's twenty-one sons. . . . Flying, then, becomes a selfish celebration of the freedom of an individual judged against the enslavement of twenty-two people" (*Fiction* 106). For Marianne Hirsch, what may be considered "[h]eroic soaring is also antiheroic evasion" (78).

14. See also Marilyn Sanders Mobley's "Call and Response," in which she views the opening scene as a foregrounding of what would happen later in the story (51).

15. See Jacqueline De Weever's "Toni Morrison's Use of Fairy Tale, Folktale and Myth in *Song of Solomon*" (131–44), and Diane Kim Bowman's "Flying High" (10–17), among others.

16. The anthology *A Treasury of Afro-American Folklore* edited by Harold Courlander documents three different accounts of flying Africans (285–86).

17. Farah Jasmine Griffin, in *"Who Set You Flowin'?": The African-American Migration Narrative,* goes further to see the song not as a history of the Dead family but as a text embodying the gamut of African American experience. In her words, "Embodied within the lyrics are a documentation of the diversity of African ethnicities and religions that converge on the American continent, the horror of fragmentation and destruction of black families and black bodies, and their economic

exploitation—all in a plea to the ancestor, Solomon, who flew off and left these bodies on these hostile shores" (176). Similarly, Susan Willis regards Milkman's quest as leading him to the discovery of the "twin texts of history: song and genealogy." "In so doing," Willis continues, "he reconstructs the dialectic of historical transition, where individual genealogy evokes the history of black migration and the chain of economic expropriation from hinterland to village, and village to metropolis" (271). On the other hand, Marc C. Conner rightly notes that Milkman's memorization of the song is an act that "brings him toward both self and communal awareness [through] an encounter with a language that defies representation," that is, writing (61). Certainly, this is a song laden with historical significance; yet its importance is attained through the agency of orality as a way of undermining the oppressive overdetermination of literacy in a society that has sought to block the African American's access to the written word.

18. See Nancy J. Peterson, "'Say Make Me, Remake Me': Toni Morrison and the Reconstruction of African-American History." Peterson argues that Morrison's notion of history is unconventional, attributable to her "improvisational exploration of alternative concepts and forms for reconstructing African-American history" (202).

19. A striking similarity exists between the youths' taunt of Esther and the didactic tale of a blind old woman and her youthful tormentors that Morrison uses to frame her Nobel Prize lecture. In each instance, the burden of proof is on the blind woman, but whereas Esther allows the fathers to exploit her privileged position as elder (and thus her presumed wisdom), the woman cited in the lecture exercises her place as conscience of her community and transforms the encounter to a positive one (see http://nobelprize.org/nobel_prizes/literature/laureates/1993/morrison-lecture.html).

20. Again, unlike Macon, who imposes his will on the contours of the letters that form his daughter's name, insisting on the name despite its oddity, Esther's "finger memory" cannot suffice. It may well suggest that Morrison grants moral power to Macon while Esther is rebuked for failing to speak truth to power.

21. Paul Connerton suggests that members of a community form communal memory through the interlocking of individual histories (16–17).

22. See Richard Bauman's *Story, Performance, and Event* (esp. 49–52) for a discussion of the narrative practice described here. The fact that Bauman's analysis pertains to oral storytelling seems to further vindicate the appropriateness of applying performance rhetoric in interpreting Deacon's speech. Morrison, too, suggests such a connection by including gestural and emphatic phrases in the twins' story.

23. Matthew 26:36–46; Mark 14:32–42; Luke 22:39–46.

24. At the Disallowing, the people of Fairly refused the trekkers residence but had provided them with supplies and money to aid them on their journey. The men, in their pride, left the items where the offer was made and continued on their journey. What the men do not know is that the women sneaked back to gather the food to feed their little children to save them from starving to death. Once the reader gets this information, it becomes clear that this is a rupture of the master narrative, or rather, that there exists an alternative narrative, surreptitiously stored in the memory of the women. This narrative remains silenced; yet

since half of the members of the 8-R (the women) know it, this alternate narrative has the potential to disrupt the men's narrative.

25. The conflict surrounding Patricia's efforts to account for those whose names have been erased from the history of Haven/Ruby seems to validate one of the "disputes" in Jean-François Lyotard's *The Differend*. The book continues Lyotard's discourse on the dialectics of "master" narratives and "local" narratives, here configured as conflict between "little stories" and "History." Using the cultural practices of the Cashinahua, Lyotard states, "The little stories received and bestowed names. The great story of history has its end in the extinction of names (particularism). At the end of the great story, there will simply be humanity" (155). In other words, it is in the interest of a hegemonic power to suppress dissent through the elimination of narratives that challenge its authoritarianism. Patricia's action of writing a different narrative falls within Lyotard's argument that "the perpetuation of narratives of origin by means of repeated narratives" is the key to the consolidation of political power (147). But so much has changed since Lyotard's definition of these terms that they have become almost opprobrium in contemporary usage. I believe that Morrison is aware of this change, and that is why she pursues Patricia's agenda guardedly.

26. Even this piece of information is inconclusive. In Patricia's view, "His [Zechariah's] foot was shot through—by whom or why nobody knew or admitted, for the point of the story seemed to be that when the bullet entered he neither cried out nor limped away" (189). This is yet another example of the novel's careful presentation of composite opinions that show the elusiveness of a single version of communal memory.

27. Isaiah 40:3.

28. I have put "other" in parentheses because even though the narrator constructs herself as a storyteller who knows her characters, the structure of the novel itself appears to disprove it. The authority of her narrative voice is considerably undermined by the insistence of the other characters to speak for themselves, oftentimes exposing the error in the narrator's presumptuousness. She, too, like her characters, is an evolving subject in the narrative. Hence, Denise Heinze correctly describes her as "a voice that is both speaker and text, the book itself" (182).

29. Michael Cooke, who has identified works that "make no bones about their business, which is black experience," has noted this tendency toward specificity in historical inquiry (210). In their quest for meaning, these works are "infused with a deliberateness and specificity of enquiry into the past that would seem to make investigation a form of action" (224).

30. It is because of this deconstruction of the narrator that Heinze refers to *Jazz* as "a metafictional fiction" (181). See also Philip Page's essay "Traces of Derrida" in which he analyzes the novel as a postmodernist work because of its avoidance of dualities and the use of elliptical phrasing of meaning, among other attributes (57).

31. Doreatha Drummond Mbalia, in "Women Who Run with Wild," bases much of her discussion of the novel on the connection of the work to the theme and structure of jazz music (623–46). Eusebia L. Rodrigues, in the same journal issue where Mbalia's essay appears, takes the analogy further through an analysis that

virtually transforms the novel into one jazz score (733–54). On the other hand, Alan Munton expressly dismisses such a comparison. "The substantive error lies in thinking of jazz as a language similar in kind to spoken human language," Munton contends. "It is true that jazz is often described as a language," he continues. "Spoken language and the 'language' of jazz differ fundamentally, and it is possible to determine the latter from the former" (235–51). See also Caroline Brown's essay in which she draws parallels between the history of jazz, its social and political impact in the United States, and the art of Morrison's *Jazz*. Fred Wei-han Ho, who sees the music as embodying both the European concert tradition and West African rhythmic patterns, takes a more pragmatic approach to the subject. Noting Morrison's interplay of written and oral forms in her works, Ho's position could be considered more reflective of Morrison's narratology.

32. I use this term in an African context where it is a taboo to unmask a masquerade in public. It is not that the identity of *Jazz*'s narrator is in dispute, but it is the "horror" a reader feels in encountering a narrator whose role in the story is called into question. The evaporation of the narrator's omniscience is akin to the unmasking of an ancestral spirit's presence in broad daylight.

33. John Young has done a remarkable job of finding in Morrison's performance of the audiobook version of *Jazz* the quintessential demonstration of the African American "talking book." Whereas part of the "tricks" in *Jazz* is the contrived intimacy between the reader and the narrator (or, physically, the book), listening to Morrison lend her voice to this narration, Young shows, returns the novel back to the oral basis of the "talking book" (196).

Chapter Five

1. See also Toomer's letter to Sherwood Anderson, where he proposes a magazine project that would "consciously hoist, and perhaps at first a trifle over emphasize a Negroid ideal. A magazine that would function organically for what I feel to be the budding of the Negro's consciousness" (Rusch, *Reader* 85). The later emergence of writers such as Claude McKay, Countee Cullen, Jessie Fauset, Nella Larsen, Zora Neale Hurston, and Langston Hughes could be seen as the blooming of this "Negroid ideal."

2. It is not clear whether in fact Byrd is punning on the common legal code found in many states during the slave era that specified that the status of a child born to a black woman even by her white master must follow the "condition of the mother."

3. See "Looking Behind *Cane*" by David Bradley for a more sympathetic interrogation of the ambiguous connection between Toomer and the Harlem Renaissance.

4. Genesis 4:15.

5. Here it is useful to recognize the recent seminal work by Chezia Thompson Cager wherein she offers a holistic reading of *Cane* based on what she calls the "Vertical Technique" (1). The approach explains the narrative sequences in *Cane* according to major moments in African American historical experience. Cager's analytical tool comes closest to capturing the organicity of *cane* because the

"Technique" is premised on two notions, first, recognizing that diaspora Africans "come from comprehensible cultures with complex linguistic forms and a repertoire of gestures that accompany those forms" (13), and, second, evoking the African concept of time, which is cyclical (13–15). The former explains the multiple forms in the text, while the latter offers a plausible explanation for *Cane*'s "plot." What is not addressed in the study is the centrality of the oral artist as "text maker" and the text, as well.

6. Because of the large presence of oral cultures in Africa, Eileen Julien, in her book on orality and African literature, has similarly pointed out a fallacy among some critics and researchers who seem to essentialize orality as an African attribute and regard writing as "disjunctive" to the African. Such critics, Julien notes, "assume almost invariably that there is something ontologically oral about Africa," a false assumption (8). On the American scene, Harryette Mullen warns that "any theory of African-American literature that privileges a speech based poetics, or the trope of orality, to the exclusion of more writerly texts will cost us some impoverishment of the tradition" (670–71).

7. There is an illuminating example of this external interjection in the personal narrative of Elizabeth Tonkin, a folklorist carrying out fieldwork among an ethnic group in Liberia. The following excerpt reveals the consequence of attempting to view the artistic exchange as other than ordinary: "In the same village as Blamo Kofo [a griot] lived Nimene Gbei, a woman who was proudly called Territory Singer, Blenyeno (song woman). . . . It was difficult to get a recording from her, since she was always busy, working on her rice farm. . . . When I persuaded her, she was obviously put out by having to perform cold, not in the ambiance of a party audience . . . and she also paused to demand money. Nevertheless, it was a thrilling performance for me, who understood few of the words. Anybody who could come to the house turned up to listen and I wish I had provided lots of drinks, but apart from costs I was troubled at the time at how I would record her audibly in party circumstances!" (45). The disappointment here is that Tonkin appears to understand the importance of capturing performance in its natural environment, but she lets economic considerations and her sense of order stifle what apparently could have been a great performance.

8. See Gerald L. Davis's *I Got the Word in Me and I Can Sing It, You Know*, where he describes phrase sermophones such as "preach it," "thank you, Jesus," and "carry me, Lord" as "generally used in a supportive manner to affirm an observation of the preacher or a particular event in the Church or sermon" (99). They also affirm the shared spiritual and social experiences between the preacher and the congregation.

9. Robert G. O'Meally defines the Amen Corner as "that section of a congregation, positioned near the pulpit, where older members sit and lead the church in responses to the service" (69–70). Most sermophones begin from the Amen Corner.

10. In a version of the African American Tar Baby folktale, the animals finally catch Rabbit and proceed to hang him. Rabbit begs them to throw him on a briar patch instead. The animals wonder why Rabbit would prefer dying under such painful circumstances, but they oblige him anyway. What the animals do not know is that the patch is a familiar tuft to Rabbit, and so when they throw him

down, he survives and scurries away laughing. Carma plays the same trick on her husband by planning the site of her feigned suicide among cane leaves, a venue that is quite familiar to her.

11. In her reading of the lyrical aspects of this story, Kimberly Banks argues that the three-line refrain ("Red nigger . . . fact'ry door") is a call for political and moral action, especially as the black community fails to rise in defense of Tom against the white lynching mob. Banks concludes her analysis by stating, "The decision to represent lynching in lyrical terms prompts readers to see lynching as a loss of social power" (463–64). Granted, Banks reads the story alongside two other texts, and her reading dwells more on the gender and racial power struggle between the two men over Louisa than a consideration of the narrative aesthetics of the text.

12. Note, for example, Okpewho's rendition of the text of two legend performances in *African Oral Literature.* Okpewho accounts for the words of the narrator, Charles Simayi, and equally includes interjections by members of the audience, side comments, laughter, murmuring, and even the whimpering of a baby in that audience as a way of conveying the event as an ongoing dialogue between the artist and his audience (183–201). In formal written drama, such inclusions would fall under the general rubric of "stage directions." Although Toomer does not format the "introductory narratives" that lead to the dialogues as such, they share an affinity with the extensive narratives on characters and settings that pass for "stage directions" in Wole Soyinka's plays.

13. Though his definition is more specific to his reading of Ngugi Wa Thiong'o's novels, F. Odun Balogun's definition and application of the term "multigenre" closely relates to the notion I am expressing here. He sees a multigenre novel as "one within which several literary genres, traditionally separated as incompatible or linked only in subordinative relationships, co-exist on equal footing, and in which, at the same time, the essential characteristics of the traditional novel . . . are carefully preserved" (5–6).

Afterword

1. Nigerian pidgin for "Were they like these?" which is practically the same in meaning as "Ever see teet' as dese?"

— WORKS CITED —

Abrahams, Roger D. *The Man-of-Words in the West Indies: Performance and the Emergence of Creole Culture.* Baltimore: Johns Hopkins University Press, 1983.

———. "Personal Power and Social Restraint in the Definition of Folklore." In Parades and Bauman, 16–30.

———. *Singing the Master: The Emergence of African American Culture in the Plantation South.* New York: Penguin, 1992.

Achebe, Chinua. "The Novelist as Teacher." In *Hopes and Impediments: Selected Essays.* New York: Doubleday/Anchor, 1989. 40–46.

———. *Things Fall Apart.* London: Heinemann, 1958.

Adedeji, Joel. "Traditional Yoruba Theater." *African Arts* 3.1 (Autumn 1969): 60–63.

Altieri, Charles. *Act and Quality: A Theory of Literary Meaning and Humanistic Understanding.* Amherst: University of Massachusetts Press, 1981.

Baker, Houston A., Jr. *Afro-American Poetics: Revisions of Harlem and the Black Aesthetic.* Madison: University of Wisconsin Press, 1988.

Bakhtin, M. M. *The Dialogic Imagination: Four Essays.* Trans. Caryl Emerson and Michael Holquist. Ed. Michael Holquist. Austin: University of Texas Press, 1981.

Baldwin, James. "The Black Scholar Interviews James Baldwin." In Standley and Pratt, 142–58.

Balogun, F. Odun. *Ngugi and African Postcolonial Narrative: The Novel as Oral Narrative in Multigenre Performance.* Quebec City: World Heritage, 1997.

Banks, Kimberly. "'Like a violin for the wind to play': Lyrical Approaches to Lynching by Hughes, DuBois, and Toomer." *African American Review* 38.3 (Fall 2004): 451–65.

Bauman, Richard. "'I'll Give You Three Guesses': The Dynamics of Genre in the Riddle-Tale." In *Untying the Knot: On Riddles and Other Enigmatic Modes.* Ed. Galit Hasan-Rokem and David Shulman. New York: Oxford University Press, 1996. 62–77.

———. *Story, Performance, and Event: Contextual Studies of Oral Narrative.* Cambridge: Cambridge University Press, 1986.

Works Cited

Ben-Amos, Dan. "Toward a Definition of Folklore in Context." In Parades and Bauman, 3–15.

Benitez-Rojo, Antonio. *The Repeating Island: The Caribbean and the Postmodern Perspective*. 2nd ed. Trans. James E. Maraniss. Durham, NC: Duke University Press, 1996.

Biakolo, Emevwho A. "Narrative Categories and Oral-Written Literary Transformations." Diss., University of Ibadan, 1987.

Black, Joel. *The Aesthetics of Murder: A Study in Romantic Literature and Contemporary Culture*. Baltimore: Johns Hopkins University Press, 1991.

Blake, Susan L. "The Spectatorial Artist and the Structure of *Cane*." *CLA Journal* 17.4 (1974): 516–34.

Bowman, Diane Kim. "Flying High: The American Icarus in Morrison, Roth, and Updike." *Perspectives on Contemporary Literature* 8 (1982): 10–17.

Bradley, David. "Looking Behind *Cane*." *Southern Review* 21.3 (1985): 682–94.

Branch, Eleanor. "Through the Mace of the Oedipal: Milkman's Search for Self in *Song of Solomon*." *Literature and Psychology* 41.1 & 2 (1995): 52–84.

Brathwaite, Kamau E. *History of the Voice: The Development of Nation Language in Anglophone Caribbean Poetry*. London: New Beacon, 1984.

———. "Jazz and the West Indian Novel, I, II, III." In *The Routledge Reader in Caribbean Literature*. Ed. Alison Donnell and Sarah Lawson Welsh. New York: Routledge, 1996. 336–53.

Breton, André. *Manifestoes of Surrealism*. Ann Arbor: University of Michigan Press, 1969.

Brown, Caroline. "Golden Gray and the Talking Book: Identity as a Site of Artful Construction in Toni Morrison's *Jazz*." *African American Review* 36.4 (2002): 629–42.

Byrd, Rudolf P. "Jean Toomer and the Afro-American Literary Tradition." *Callaloo* 8.2 (1985): 310–19.

Cager, Chezia Thompson. *Teaching Jean Roomer's 1923* Cane. New York: Lang, 2006.

Calder, Alder. "An Audience with C. L. R. James." *Third World Book Review* 1.2 (1984): 6–8.

Cannon, Elizabeth M. "Following the Traces of Female Desire in Toni Morrison's *Jazz*." *African American Review* 31.2 (1997): 235–47.

Carpentier, Alejo. "On the Marvelous Real in America." In *Magical Realism: Theory, History, Community*. Ed. with Introduction by Lois Parkinson Zamora and Wendy B. Faris. Durham, NC: Duke University Press, 1995. 75–88.

Cartey, Wilfred. *Whispers from the Caribbean: I Going Away, I Going Home*. Los Angeles: Center for Afro-American Studies, University of California, 1991.

Carvalho-Neto, Paulo de. *The Concept of Folklore*. 1965. Trans. Jacques M. P. Wilson. Coral Gables, FL: University of Miami Press, 1971.

Chesneaux, Jean. *Pasts and Futures or What Is History For?* Trans. Schofield Coryell. London: Thames and Hudson, 1978.

Conner, Marc C. "From the Sublime to the Beautiful: The Aesthetic Progression of Toni Morrison." In *The Aesthetics of Toni Morrison: Speaking the Unspeakable*. Ed. Marc C. Conner. Jackson: University Press of Mississippi, 2000. 49–76.

Connerton, Paul. *How Societies Remember*. Cambridge: Cambridge University Press, 1989.

Cooke, Michael G. *African American Literature in the Twentieth Century: The Achievement of Intimacy.* New Haven, CT: Yale University Press, 1984.

Courlander, Harold, ed. *A Treasury of Afro-American Folklore: The Oral Literature, Traditions, Recollections, Legends, Tales, Songs, Religious Beliefs, Customs, Sayings and Humor of Peoples of African Descent in the Americas.* 1976. New York: Smithmark, 1996.

Creighton, Al. "The Human Comedy: Carnival and the Infinite Rehearsal." In Maes-Jelinek, *Wilson Harris,* 192–99.

Cudjoe, Selwyn R. *Resistance and Caribbean Literature.* Athens: Ohio University Press, 1980.

Cullen, Countee, ed. *Caroling Dusk: An Anthology of Verse by Negro Poets.* New York: Harper and Brothers, 1927.

D'Aguiar, Fred. "Interview with Wilson Harris." *Bomb* 82 (Winter 2002/2003): 74–80.

Danow, David K. *The Spirit of Carnival: Magical Realism and the Grotesque.* Lexington: University Press of Kentucky, 1995.

Dash, J. Michael. *The Other America: Caribbean Literature in a New World Context.* Charlottesville: University Press of Virginia, 1998.

Davis, Gerald L. *I Got the Word in Me and I Can Sing It, You Know: A Study of the Performed African-American Sermon.* Philadelphia: University of Pennsylvania Press, 1985.

Davies, Carole Boyce. *Black Women, Writing and Identity: Migrations of the Subject.* London: Routledge, 1994.

Derrida, Jacques. *Positions.* Trans. and annotated by Alan Bass. Chicago: University of Chicago Press, 1982.

De Weever, Jacqueline. "Toni Morrison's Use of Fairy Tale, Folktale and Myth in *Song of Solomon.*" *Southern Folklore Quarterly* 44 (1980): 131–44.

Dieke, Ikenna. *The Primordial Image: African, Afro-American and Caribbean Mythopoetic Text.* New York: Peter Lang, 1993.

Dorsey, David. "Prolegomena for Black Aesthetics." In *Black Aesthetics: Papers from a Colloquium Held at the University of Nairobi, June 1971.* Ed. Andrew Gurr and Pio Zirimu. Nairobi: East Africa Literature Bureau, 1973. 7–19.

Drake, Sandra. *Wilson Harris and the Modern Tradition: A New Architecture of the World.* New York: Greenwood, 1986.

DuBois, W. E. B. *The Souls of Black Folk.* Introduction by John Edgar Wideman. New York: Vintage and Library of America, 1990.

Duncan, Bowie. "Jean Toomer's Cane: A Modern Black Oracle." *CLA Journal* 15.3 (1972): 323–33.

Dundes, Alan. *Interpreting Folklore.* Bloomington: Indiana University Press, 1980.

Dutch, William L. "Three Enigmas: Karintha, Becky, and Carma." In O'Daniel, 265–68.

Duvall, John N. *The Identifying Fictions of Toni Morrison: Modernist Authenticity and Postmodern Blackness.* New York: Palgrave, 2000.

Echeruo, Michael J. C. "An African Diaspora: the Ontological Project." In *The African Diaspora: African Origins and New World Identities.* Ed. Isidore Okpewho, Carole Boyce Davies, and Ali A. Mazrui. Bloomington: Indiana University Press, 1999. 3–18.

Works Cited

Erdelyi, Matthew Hugh. *The Recovery of Unconscious Memories.* Chicago: University of Chicago Press, 1996.

Farrison, W. Edward. "Jean Toomer's *Cane* Again." *CLA Journal* 15.3 (1972): 295–302.

Feder, Lillian. *Madness in Literature.* Princeton, NJ: Princeton University Press, 1980.

Finnegan, Ruth. *Literacy and Orality: Studies in the Technology of Communication.* New York: Basil Blackwell, 1988.

Foley, Barbara. "Jean Toomer's Washington and the Politics of Class: From 'Blue Veins' to Seventh-Street Rebels." *Modern Fiction Studies* 42.2 (1996): 289–321.

Forster, E. M. *Aspects of the Novel.* New York: Harcourt, 1924.

Foucault, Michel. *Madness and Civilization: A History of Insanity in the Age of Reason.* Trans. Richard Howard. New York: Vintage, 1973.

Gates, Henry Louis, Jr. *The Signifying Monkey: Toward A Theory of Afro-American Literary Criticism.* New York: Oxford University Press, 1988.

Gates, Henry Louis, Jr., and Nellie Y. McKay, eds. *The Norton Anthology of African American Literature.* New York: Norton, 1997.

Gilroy, Paul. *The Black Atlantic: Modernity and Double Consciousness.* Cambridge, MA: Harvard University Press, 1993.

——. *Small Acts: Thoughts on the Politics of Black Cultures.* London: Serpent's Tail, 1993.

Goody, Jack. *The Domestication of the Savage Mind.* Cambridge: Cambridge University Press, 1977.

——. *The Interface Between the Written and the Oral.* New York: Cambridge University Press, 1987.

Griffin, Farah Jasmine. *"Who Set You Flowin'?": The African-American Migration Narrative.* New York: Oxford University Press, 1995.

Griffiths, Gareth. "Post-Colonial Space and Time and Caribbean Criticism." In Maes-Jelinek, *Wilson Harris,* 61–69.

Gruesser, John Cullen. *Confluences: Postcolonialism, African American Literary Studies, and the Black Atlantic.* Athens: University of Georgia Press, 2005.

Hajek, Friederike. "The Change of Literary Authority in the Harlem Renaissance: Jean Toomer's *Cane.*" In Sollors and Diedrich, 185–90.

Hall, Gwendolyn Midlo. *Slavery and African Ethnicities in the Americas: Restoring the Links.* Chapel Hill: University of North Carolina Press, 2005.

Hamlet, Desmond. "Sustaining the Vision: Wilson Harris and the Uncompromising Imagination." In Maes-Jelinek, *Wilson Harris,* 200–209.

Harris, Trudier. *Fiction and Folklore: The Novels of Toni Morrison.* Knoxville: University of Tennessee Press, 1991.

——. *The Power of the Porch: The Storyteller's Craft in Zora Neale Hurston, Gloria Naylor, and Randall Kenan.* Athens: University of Georgia Press, 1996.

Harris, Wilson. *Carnival.* 1985. *The Carnival Trilogy.* Introduction by Wilson Harris. London: Faber and Faber, 1993.

——. "Closing Statement: Apprenticeship to the Furies." In *Comparing Post-colonial Literatures.* Ed. Ashok Berry and Patricia Murray. London: Macmillan, 2000. 240–51.

——. *The Dark Jester.* London: Faber and Faber, 2001.

———. "History, Fable and Myth in the Caribbean and Guianas." In *Selected Essays,* 152–66.

———. *Jonestown.* London: Faber and Faber, 1996.

———. "The Landscape of Dream." Conversation with Michael Gilkes. In Maes-Jelinek, *Wilson Harris,* 31–38.

———. "Literacy and the Imagination—A Talk." In *Selected Essays,* 75–89.

———. *Palace of the Peacock.* The Guyana Quartet. London: Faber and Faber, 1985.

———. *Resurrection at Sorrow Hill.* London: Faber and Faber, 1993.

———. *Selected Essays of Wilson Harris: The Unfinished Genesis of the Imagination.* Ed. A. J. M. Bundy. London: Routledge, 1999.

———. "Tradition and the West Indian Novel." In *Selected Essays,* 140–51.

———. "Wilson Harris." *Contemporary Authors: Autobiography Series,* vol. 6. Detroit, MI: Gale Research Group, 1992.

———. *The Womb of Space: The Cross-Cultural Imagination.* Westport, CT: Greenwood, 1983.

———. "The Writer and Society." In *Tradition, the Writer and Society: Critical Essays.* Ed. Wilson Harris. London: New Beacon, 1967. 48–64.

Hart, Robert C. "Black-White Literary Relations in the Harlem Renaissance." *American Literature* 44.4 (1973): 612–28.

Havelock, Eric A. *Preface to Plato.* Cambridge, MA: Belknap Press/Harvard University Press, 1963.

Heath, Roy A. K. "Continuing Colonialism." Interview with Frank Birbalsingh. In *Frontiers of Caribbean Literature in English.* Ed. Frank Birbalsingh. New York: St. Martin's, 1996. 68–85.

———. "The Function of Myth." In *Caribbean Essays.* Ed. Andrew Salkey. London: Evans, 1972. 86–94.

———. *Kwaku or the Man Who Could Not Keep His Mouth Shut.* London: Allison and Busby, 1982.

———. *A Man Come Home.* London: Longman Group Limited, 1974.

———. *The Ministry of Hope.* New York: Marion Boyars, 1997.

———. *The Murderer.* London: Allison and Busby, 1978. New York: Persea, 1992.

———. *Orealla.* London: Allison and Busby, 1984.

———. *The Shadow Bride.* London: William Collins, 1988. New York: Persea, 1996.

Heinze, Denise. *The Dilemma of 'Double Consciousness': Toni Morrison's Novels.* Athens: University of Georgia Press, 1993.

Hirsch, Marianne. "Knowing Their Names: Toni Morrison's *Song of Solomon.*" In Smith, 69–92.

Ho, Fred Wei-han. "What Makes 'Jazz' the Revolutionary Music of the 20th Century, and Will It Be Revolutionary for the 21st Century?" *African American Review* 29.12 (1995): 283–90.

Hogue, W. Lawrence. *Race, Modernity, Postmodernity: A Look at the History and the Literatures of Peoples of Color Since the 1960s.* Albany: State University of New York Press, 1996.

Homer. *The Odyssey.* Trans. Robert Fitzgerald. New York: Random/Vintage, 1990.

"Horror Lives On: A Search for Answers to the Questions of Jonestown." *Time,* 11 Dec. 1978: 28.

Hughes, Langston. "The Negro Artist and the Racial Mountain." In Gates and McKay, 1267–71.

Works Cited

Ikonne, Chidi. *From DuBois to Van Vechten: The Early New Negro Literature, 1903-1926.* Westport, CT: Greenwood, 1981.

Irele, Abiola. "The African Imagination." *Research in African Literatures* 21.1 (Spring 1990): 49-67.

John, Catherine A. *Clear Word and Third Sight: Folk Groundings and Diasporic Consciousness in African Caribbean Writing.* Durham, NC: Duke University Press, 2003.

Jones, Gayl. *Liberating Voices: Oral Tradition in African American Literature.* New York: Penguin, 1992.

Jones, Robert B., ed. with Introduction. *Jean Toomer and the Prison-House of Thought: A Phenomenology of the Spirit.* Amherst: University of Massachusetts Press, 1993.

——. *Jean Toomer: Selected Essays and Literary Criticism.* Knoxville: University of Tennessee Press, 1996.

Julien, Eileen. *African Novels and the Question of Orality.* Bloomington: Indiana University Press, 1992.

Kirk, G. S. *Myth.* Cambridge: Cambridge University Press, 1975.

Klein, Kerwin Lee. "In Search of Narrative Mastery: Postmodernism and the People Without History." *History and Theory: Studies in the Philosophy of History* 34.4 (1995): 275-98.

Kraft, James. "Jean Toomer's *Cane.*" In O'Daniel, 147-52.

Larson, Charles R. "*Cane* by Jean Toomer." *New Republic*, 19 June 1976: 30-32.

Lehmann, Elmar. "Remembering the Past: Toni Morrison's Version of the Historical Novel." In *Lineages of the Novel: Essays in Honour of Raimund Borgmeier.* Ed. Berhard Reitz and Eckart Voigts-Virchow. Trier, Germany: WVT, 2000. 197-203.

Lidinsky, April. "Prophesying Bodies: Calling for a Politics of Collectivity in Toni Morrison's *Beloved.*" In *The Discourse of Slavery: Aphra Behn to Toni Morrison.* Ed. Carl Plasa and Betty J. Ring. New York: Routledge, 1994. 191-216.

Lieber, Todd. "Design and Movement in *Cane.*" In O'Daniel, 179-93.

Lipsitz, George. "Myth, History, and Counter-Memory." In *Politics and the Muse: Studies in the Politics of Recent American Literature.* Ed. Adam J. Sorkin. Bowling Green, OH: Bowling Green State University Popular Press, 1989. 161-78.

Lord, Albert B. *The Singer of Tales.* Cambridge, MA: Harvard University Press, 1960.

Locke, Alain. "The New Negro." In *The New Negro: An Interpretation.* Ed. Alain Locke. New York: Arno Press and the New York Times, 1968. 3-16.

Lovelace, Earl. *The Dragon Can't Dance.* Essex, UK: Longman, 1981.

Lucente, Gregory L. *The Narrative of Realism and Myth: Verga, Lawrence, Faulkner, Pavese.* Baltimore: Johns Hopkins University Press, 1981.

Lyotard, Jean-François. *The Differend: Phrases in Dispute.* Trans. Georges Van Den Abbeele. Minneapolis: University of Minnesota Press, 1988.

MacKinnon, Catherine. *Toward a Feminist Theory of the State.* Cambridge, MA: Harvard University Press, 1989.

Maes-Jelinek, Hena. "'Carnival' and Creativity in Wilson Harris's Fiction." In *The Literate Imagination: Essays on the Novels of Wilson Harris.* Ed. Michael Gilkes. London: Macmillan, 1989. 45-61.

——. *The Labyrinth of Universality: Wilson Harris's Visionary Art of Fiction.* New York: Rodopi, 2006.

——. "Wilson Harris." In *West Indian Literature.* Ed. Bruce King. Hamden, CT: Archon, 1979. 179-95.

———, ed. *Wilson Harris: The Uncompromising Imagination*. Sydney: Dangaroo, 1991.

Mbalia, Doreatha Drummond. "Women Who Run with Wild: The Need for Sisterhood in *Jazz*." *Modern Fiction Studies* 39.3 & 4 (1993): 623–46.

McKay, Nellie. "An Interview with Toni Morrison." In *Toni Morrison: Critical Perspectives Past and Present*. Ed. Henry Louis Gates, Jr., and K. A. Appiah. New York: Amistad Press, 1993. 396–411.

McWatt, Mark A. "Wives and Other Victims: Women in the Novels of Roy A. K. Heath." In *Out of the Kumbla: Caribbean Women and Literature*. Ed. Carole Boyce Davies and Elaine Savory Fido. Trenton, NJ: Africa World, 1990. 223–35.

Mobley, Marilyn Sanders. "Call and Response: Voice, Community, and Dialogic Structures in Toni Morrison's *Song of Solomon*." In Smith, 41–68.

Morrison, Toni. *Beloved*. New York: Penguin-Plume, 1987.

———. Interview with Cecil Brown. *Massachusetts Review* 36 (1995): 455–73.

———. *Jazz*. New York: Penguin-Plume, 1993.

———. "Memory, Creation and Writing." *Thought* 59 (1984): 385–90.

———. "Nobel Lecture."

In *Nobel Lectures, Literature 1991–1995*. Ed. Sture Allén. Singapore: World Scientific Publishing Co., 1997. http://nobelprize.org/nobel_prizes/literature/laureates/1993/morrison-lecture.html.

———. *Paradise*. New York: Knopf, 1998.

———. *Playing in the Dark: Whiteness and the Literary Imagination*. Cambridge, MA: Harvard University Press, 1992.

———. "Rootedness: The Ancestor as Foundation." In *Black Women Writers (1950–1980)*. Ed. Mari Evans. New York: Anchor/Doubleday, 1984. 339–45.

———. *Song of Solomon*. New York: Plume-Penguin, 1977.

———. *Tar Baby*. New York: Penguin-Plume, 1982.

———. "Unspeakable Things Unspoken: The Afro-American Presence in American Literature." In *Criticism and the Color Line: Desegregating American Literary Studies*. Ed. Henry B. Wonham. New Brunswick, NJ: Rutgers University Press, 1996. 16–29.

Mullen, Harryette Romell. "African Signs and Spirit Writing." *Callaloo* 19.3 (1996): 670–89.

Munson, Gorham B. "The Significance of Jean Toomer." *Opportunity* 3.33 (1925): 262.

Munton, Alan. "Misreading Morrison, Mishearing *Jazz*: A Response to Toni Morrison's *Jazz* Critics." *Journal of American Studies* 31.2 (1997): 235–51.

Nora, Pierre. "Between Memory and History: Les Lieux de Mémoire." Trans. Marc Roudebush. In *History and Memory in African-American Culture*. Ed. Genevieve Fabre and Robert O'Meally. New York: Oxford University Press, 1994. 284–300.

O'Daniel, Therman B. *Jean Toomer: A Critical Evaluation*. Washington, DC: Howard University Press, 1988.

Ogunba, Oyin. "Traditional African Festival Drama." In *Theatre in Africa*. Ed. Oyin Ogunba and Abiola Irele. Ibadan, Nigeria: Ibadan University Press, 1978. 3–26.

Okpewho, Isidore. *African Oral Literature: Backgrounds, Character, and Continuity*. Bloomington: Indiana University Press, 1992.

———. "The Cousins of Uncle Remus." In Sollors and Diedrich, 15–27.

Works Cited

———. *The Epic in Africa: Toward a Poetics of the Oral Performance.* New York: Columbia University Press, 1979.

———. *Myth in Africa: A Study of Its Aesthetic and Cultural Relevance.* Cambridge: Cambridge University Press, 1983.

O'Meally, Robert G. "Sermons." In Gates and McKay, 69–70.

O'Neal, John. "Black Arts: Notebook." In *The Black Aesthetic.* Ed. Addison Gayle, Jr. New York: Doubleday, 1971. 47–58.

Ong, Walter J. *Interfaces of the Word: Studies in the Evolution of Consciousness and Culture.* Ithaca, NY: Cornell University Press, 1977.

———. *Orality and Literacy.* London: Methuen, 1982.

Page, Philip. "Traces of Derrida in Toni Morrison's *Jazz.*" *African American Review* 29.1 (1995): 55–66.

Parades, Americo, and Richard Bauman, eds. *Toward New Perspectives in Folklore.* Austin: University of Texas for American Folklore Society, 1972.

Paravisini-Gebert, Lizabeth. "Writers Playin' Mas': Carnival and the Grotesque in the Contemporary Caribbean Novel." In *A History of Literature in the Caribbean.* Ed. A. James Arnold. Vol. 3. Amsterdam: John Benjamin, 1997. 215–36.

Peterson, Nancy J. "'Say Make Me, Remake Me': Toni Morrison and the Reconstruction of African-American History." In *Toni Morrison: Critical and Theoretical Approaches.* Ed. Nancy J. Peterson. Baltimore: Johns Hopkins University Press, 1997. 201–21.

Phillips, Forbes. "Ancestral Memory: A Suggestion." *Nineteenth Century* 59 (1906): 977–83.

Ramchand, Kenneth. *The West Indian Novel and Its Background.* Kingston, Jamaica: Ian Randle Publishers, 2004.

Randall-Tsuruta, Dorothy. "In Dialogue to Define Aesthetics: James Baldwin and Chinua Achebe." In Standley and Pratt, 210–21.

Riach, Alan. "The Presence of Actual Angels: The Fractal Poetics of Wilson Harris." *Callaloo* 18.1 (1995): 34–44.

Rice, Herbert William. *Toni Morrison and the American Tradition: A Rhetorical Reading.* New York: Peter Lang, 1996.

———. "Two Work Songs in *Cane.*" *Black American Literature Forum* 23.3 (1989): 593–99.

Rodrigues, Eusebia L. "Experiencing *Jazz.*" *Modern Fiction Studies* 39.3 & 4 (1993): 733–54.

Rowell, Charles H. "An Interview with Wilson Harris." *Callaloo* 18.1 (1995): 192–200.

Rusch, Frederik L. "Form, Function, and Creative Tension in *Cane*: Jean Toomer and the Need for the Avant-Garde." *MELUS* 17.14 (1991–1992): 15–28.

———, ed. *A Jean Toomer Reader: Selected Unpublished Writings.* New York: Oxford University Press, 1993.

Rushdy, Ashraf H. A. "'Rememory': Primal Scenes and Constructions in Toni Morrison's Novels." *Contemporary Literature* 31.3 (1990): 300–323.

Saakana, Amon Saba. *Colonization and the Destruction of the Mind: Psychosocial Issues of Race, Class, Religion and Sexuality in the Novels of Roy Heath.* London: Karnak House, 1996.

Schneider, Mark A. *Culture and Enchantment.* Chicago: University of Chicago Press, 1993.

Scruggs, Charles W. "The Mark of Cain and the Redemption of Art: A Study in Theme and Structure of Jean Toomer's *Cane.*" *American Literature* 41.2 (1972): 276–91.

Sekoni, Ropo. *Folk Poetics: A Sociosemiotic Study of Yoruba Trickster Tales.* Westport, CT: Greenwood, 1994.

Seydou, Christiane. "A Few Reflections on Narrative Structures of Epic Texts: A Case Example of Bambara and Fulani Epics." Trans. Brunhilde Biebuyk. *Research in African Literatures* 14.3 (Fall 1983): 312–31.

Smith, Valerie, ed. *New Essays on* Song of Solomon. Cambridge: Cambridge University Press, 1995.

Smitherman, Geneva. *Talkin and Testifyin: The Language of Black America.* Detroit, MI: Wayne State University Press, 1977.

Sollors, Werner, and Maria Diedrich, eds. *The Black Columbiad: Defining Moments in African American Literature and Culture.* Cambridge, MA: Harvard University Press, 1994.

Soyinka, Wole. *The Interpreters.* London: Heinemann, 1965.

——. *Myth, Literature and the African World.* Cambridge: Cambridge University Press, 1976. New York: Canto, 1990.

Spanos, William V. *Heidegger and Criticism: Retrieving the Cultural Politics of Destruction.* Minneapolis: University of Minnesota Press, 1993.

Standley, Fred L., and Louis H. Pratt, eds. *Conversations with James Baldwin.* Literary Conversations Series. Jackson: University Press of Mississippi, 1989.

Tally, Justine. "Reality and Discourse in Toni Morrison's Trilogy: Testing the Limits." In *Literature and Ethnicity in the Cultural Borderlands.* Ed. Jesus Benito and Anna Maria Manzanas. New York: Rodopi, 2002. 35–49.

Tonkin, Elizabeth. "Oracy and the Disguises of Literacy." In *Discourse and Its Disguises: The Interpretation of African Oral Texts.* Ed. Karin Barber and P. F. de Moraes Farias. Birmingham, UK: Centre of West African Studies, 1989. 39–48.

Toomer, Jean. *Cane.* Introduction by Darwin T. Turner. 1923. New York: Liveright, 1975.

——. "The Crock of Problems." In R. Jones, *Selected Essays,* 55–59.

——. "The Function of the Writer." In R. Jones, *Selected Essays,* 44.

——. "Letter to *The Liberator.*" In Rusch, *Reader,* 15–16.

——. "Letter to Sherwood Anderson." In Rusch, *Reader,* 85–86.

——. "The Negro Emergent." In R. Jones, *Selected Essays,* 47–54.

Torres-Saillant, Silvio. *Caribbean Poetics: Toward an Aesthetic of West Indian Literature.* Cambridge: Cambridge University Press, 1997.

Turner, Darwin T., ed. *The Wayward and the Seeking: A Collection of Writings by Jean Toomer.* Washington, DC: Howard University Press, 1982.

Twagilimana, Aimable. *Race and Gender in the Making of an African American Literary Tradition.* New York: Gartand Publishers, 1997.

Watt, Ian. *The Rise of the Novel: Studies in Defoe, Richardson and Fielding.* Berkeley: University of California Press, 1960.

Webb, Barbara J. *Myth and History in Caribbean Fiction: Alejo Carpentier, Wilson Harris, and Edouard Glissant.* Amherst: University of Massachusetts Press, 1992.

"What Is the Best Work of American Fiction of the Last 25 Years?" *New York Times,* 21 May 2006. http://www.nytimes.com/2006/05/21/books/fiction-25-years.html?ex=1156046400&en=f902fa6a21921563&ei=5070)#.

Works Cited

Whyde, Janet M. "Mediating Forms: Narrating the Body in Jean Toomer's *Cane*." *Southern Literary Journal* 26.1 (1993): 42–53.

Williams, Mark, and Alan Riach. "Reading Wilson Harris." In Maes-Jelinek, *Wilson Harris*, 51–60.

Willis, Susan. "Eruptions of Funk: Historicizing Toni Morrison." In *Black Literature and Literary Theory*. Ed. Henry Louis Gates, Jr. New York: Routledge, 1990. 263–83.

Wise, Christopher. "Nyama and Heka: African Concepts of the Word." *Comparative Literature Studies* 43.1–2 (2006): 19–38.

Yates, Frances A. *The Art of Memory*. Chicago: University of Chicago Press, 1966.

Young, John. "Toni Morrison, Oprah Winfrey, and Postmodern Popular Audiences." *African American Review* 35.2 (2001): 181–204.

Zinn, Howard. *The Politics of History*. Boston: Beacon, 1970.

— INDEX —

www.ingramcontent.com/pod-product-compliance
Lightning Source LLC
Chambersburg PA
CBHW021331090426
42742CB00008B/563